C000173745

THE ILLUSTRATED HISTORY OF
BASINGSTOKE

Basingstoke Town Hall, photographed during the 1902 Coronation ceremony.

THE ILLUSTRATED HISTORY OF
BASINGSTOKE

ARTHUR ATTWOOD
MBE

breedon **books**
PUBLISHING

First published in Great Britain in 2001 by
The Breedon Books Publishing Company Limited
Breedon House, 3 The Parker Centre, Derby, DE21 4SZ.

Sir Alan Cobham landed at Oakridge for pleasure flights. He was the pioneer
airman on the South African flight.

ISBN 1 85983 271 7

Printed and bound by Butler & Tanner, Frome, Somerset, England.

Jacket printing by GreenShires, Leicester, England.

CONTENTS

ACKNOWLEDGEMENTS

Mrs Barbara Applin for providing maps.
Robert Brown for photographs.

Basingstoke Gazette for photographs
and for supporting the project.

To my son Robin for computerising
the copy.

To Robin and his wife Lynne for
providing accommodation which
included an office at their Brading,
Isle of Wight home.

To Basingstoke and Deane Borough
Council for information.

I would also like to thank the publishers
for their excellent co-operation.

INTRODUCTION

THE LAST comprehensive history of Basingstoke, still recognised as a standard work, was Baigent and Millard's *History of Basingstoke* published in 1889. My forbear, Mr J.S. Attwood, assisted in the publication and his work in connection with the index was described as 'elaborately and carefully prepared'. He received an apology for the necessity of restricting the number of pages which compelled the joint authors to omit his alphabetical list of the inscriptions on the grave stones and tombs at the Holy Ghost Liten.

This connection with my family and the great amount of research I have undertaken during the past 25 years has provided me with the incentive to publish another such history to commemorate the beginning of a new millennium.

Contrary to the belief held by many people that Basingstoke has little historical background, the following pages will prove otherwise. Born in Basingstoke to a family with a 500-year history and being very proud of my town, and having been made one of two Freemen of Basingstoke, I owe it to my many friends and those innumerable readers who read my weekly *Gazette* articles in such favourable light. My wish is that this book will be of great help, both to the older citizens and those learning in our schools and colleges.

I have seen Basingstoke grow from a meagre population of 11,000 to nearly 100,000. If the area administered by the Basingstoke and Deane Borough Council is taken into account, then the population is over 150,000. May those host of newcomers, many from London, find this volume helpful in developing a sense of belonging.

To make this book possible I owe much to the *Basingstoke Gazette* for the opportunity given me as a journalist, to concentrate on the historical work connected with my local newspaper and for the use of the paper's records going back to 1878.

Arthur Attwood, MBE

Population of Basingstoke

1802	2,589
1811	2,656
1821	3,165
1831	3,581
1841	4,066
1851	4,263
1861	4,654
1871	5,574
1881	6,681
1891	7,960
1901	9,793
1911	11,540
1921	12,723
1931	13,865
1941 (1946)	15,850
1951	16,978
1961	25,940
1971	52,000
1981 (1982)	67,500*
1991	77,837

*With the rapid expansion under the overspill scheme, these figures are only approximate.

Horses making their way homewards through the grounds of Park Prewett.

The Holy Ghost School ruins.

EARLY BEGINNINGS

THE QUESTION I am most frequently asked is 'Where did Basingstoke get its name from?' Allied to this is the question of why such a place as Basing, the forerunner of Basingstoke, existed.

Experts in geology will tell you that Great Britain has not always been an island. Around 12,000 years ago it was joined to the continent of Europe. Melt water from the last Ice Age eventually caused sea levels to rise and severed the link. Gravel found on Hazeley Heath, close to where Bramshill Police College stands, exactly matches material from the Alps, and geologists think that it must have been washed down from those mountains before Great Britain became a separate island.

When England was connected to what is now France, ancient tribes from Europe were able to make their way across southern England. Some chose the site of Basing as a likely settlement. There was water there, and rising ground to afford protection. It was first thought that these early settlers were of the Basinga tribe (hence the title of Basing Parish Magazine). However, it is now believed that the tribe was called the Basa. But why was 'stoke' added on to the title? An ancient meaning of the word 'stoke' is 'an area added on to another'. It seems likely that the original Basing settlement became too populous, so families moved west to make a new community. The area was ideal, for water was in abundance from the River Loddon and what was to become the town was sheltered by hills.

One early settlement in the area dates from the Iron Age, a fort at Winklebury, which is now the site of Fort Hill School. Those early settlers at Winklebury, known at one time as Winklowbury, came from the ancient people living on Salisbury Plain at places such as Stonehenge. Years later, after the Roman invasion, the Romans built a road from Southampton and Winchester to Silchester, which passed within a few hundred yards of the Iron Age fort.

One of the earliest tracks in the area was the Ox Drove, west of

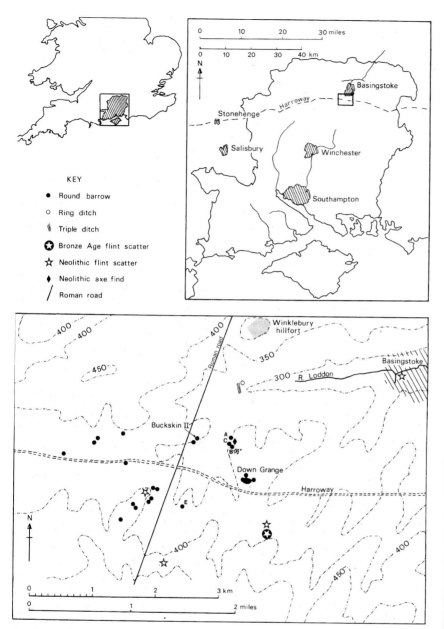

KEY

- Round barrow
- Ring ditch
- Triple ditch
- Bronze Age flint scatter
- Neolithic flint scatter
- Neolithic axe find
- Roman road

Maps from p.159 Prehistoric Society proceedings.

Basingstoke, signs of which can be found crossing a field near Oakley Church and which has been found to continue across open country from the west end of Park Prewett hospital cemetery, off the Kingsclere Road. This track once led across the Cotswolds, as far as Wales.

The Roman city of Calleva Atrebatum at Silchester, only 10 miles from Basingstoke, was occupied by the Romans for nearly 350 years. Several excavations have taken place there, the first during the closing years of the 19th century. Many artefacts were discovered, the majority of which are now in Reading Museum. The most surprising feature

The Roman road at Kempshott, a thoroughfare which ran parallel to the original road.

connected with the ruins was the discovery in 1892 of a small building measuring only 42 feet by 33 feet, planned like a church.

In the historical notes compiled by L.F. Rushbrook Williams to be found in the booklet on the Church of St Mary the Virgin, Silchester, we learn that in 1961 there was a very thorough examination of the site by the late Professor Sir Ian Richmond and Mr George Boon. They were both convinced that the building was, in fact, a Christian church. If so, Silchester would possess the earliest known urban Christian church anywhere north of the Alps. The church would date from 200 years before St Augustine supposedly brought Christianity to England in 597.

During Anglo-Saxon times (roughly AD410–1066), several early settlements were made in Basingstoke – at Oakridge to the north and Buckskin to the west, and to the east and south at Ructstall Hill, Black Dam and Viables. Our knowledge of these comes from the fine work and excavations of the Basingstoke Archaelogical Society.

Battles were fought at Basingstoke between the Danes and Saxons in 871. One site was near Oakley, where the railway to the west of England passes under Battledown flyover, which is aptly named. At Lychpit, close to Old Basing, is the site of another battle, and there is yet another battleground just over a mile to the south in the Tunworth Road area. Doubt exists about whether Lychpit is named after the burial ground for those killed in the Dane-Saxon encounter, or for those who died of the plague. The terrible 14th-century epidemic killed many in the area, particularly at Kingsclere, Baughurst and Sherfield-on-Loddon.

The area also had connections with the plague of 1665. North of Basingstoke and to the west near Andover are two villages named Little London, where those who had escaped the plague in London set up new communities.

Statements in Domesday Book of 1086 with meanings of words

'The King holds in demesne Basingstoches. It has always been a royal manor. It never paid tax nor was divided into hides. The land contains 20 ploughlands. There are three ploughlands in demesne and 20 villeins and 8 boors with 12 teams. There are 6 serfs and 3 mills which pay 30 shillings, and 12 freedmen with 4 ploughlands. There is a market paying 20 shillings, and 20 acres of meadow.'

'The three manors of Basingstoches, Clere (Kingsclere) and Essebourne (Hurstbourne) pay one day's firm (contribute the amount of one day's entertainment for the King). The Church of St Michael on the Mount holds of the King one Church with one hide, and the tithe of the manor of Basingstoches. One priest is there, and two villeins, and four boors with one ploughland, and a mill let at 20 shillings, and two acres of meadow. The whole is worth 4 pounds and 5 shillings. Bishop Walter held the land under King Edward, but it did not belong to his bishopric.'

A ploughland was sufficient to employ 20 teams of oxen. Villeins were labourers on the manor. Boors (bordarii) were a class inferior to the villains. Freedmen (colibertii) were a particular class of tenants or occupiers. The average hide consisted of about 145 acres of profitable or 255 acres of unprofitable land.

A demesne was a manor house with lands adjacent to it, not let out to tenants, or any estate in land.

In 1203 market day in Basingstoke changed from Sunday to Monday. In 1214 it changed again, from Monday to Wednesday.

MEDIÆVAL BASINGSTOKE

B Y THE 11th century, there was a Church of St Michael in existence in Basingstoke, but not the present one. In 1061, Walter, who was rector of Basingstoke, was consecrated bishop of Hereford at Rome by Pope Nicholas II.

The Abbot and Convent of Mount St Michael owned the possessions and revenues of the bishopric of Winchester, which consisted of three churches, one in the town of Basingstoke and two belonging to the monks of Mount St Michael. This led to St Michael becoming the patron saint of Basingstoke.

The area including Basing church and St Michael's Basingstoke was designated a province. The living was converted into a benefice when it was given to Selborne Priory. In Basingstoke there was no rectory as such until the beginning of the 18th century. Prior to this, from 1540 onwards, the parish priest had lived in part of Church Cottage. Until 1865, Basing church and parish came under St Michael's Basingstoke.

The gift of St Michael's Church by a charter, dated 20 January 1233, was granted to the prior and convent of Selborne for ever, but in 1486, the priory was dissolved by a Bull of Pope Innocent VIII and its possessions transferred to Magdalen College, Oxford, which still retains the benefice. In 1499 Magdalen College appointed its first rector to Basingstoke.

In the 11th century, Basingstoke was a very small place. The layout of the town was altered when an interdict was passed which prevented anyone being buried in consecrated ground. This was in 1208 and lasted until 1215 when King John made peace with the barons and the Church with the signing of Magna Carta at Runnymede. King John rode from his castle at Odiham in Hampshire to Runnymede. Meanwhile, the church in Basingstoke had to find a temporary burial place.

At that time, there was a rising hill to the north of the town covered by greensward, and this was the spot chosen. After the interdict was lifted, the populace wished to have a chapel near to where their loved ones were buried and the chapel of the Holy Ghost was built. The ruins of part of it can still be seen today.

Most of the ruins on the site of the chapel, however, are those of the Chapel of the Holy Trinity erected by

Drawing made in 1800 of the view of Basingstoke from the South View cemetery.

Lord Sandys at the beginning of Henry VIII's reign. Lord Sandys, who also built The Vyne, a nearby mansion, built the added chapel as a burial place for his family. Visitors to the ruined chapel can see two box memorials bearing the arms of the Sandys family, the cross ruglys and a winged goat.

To return to earlier times, the building of the original chapel was followed by another important event, the building of the Hospital of St John the Baptist at the bottom of Church Street. It was constructed by one of Basingstoke's famous sons, Walter de Merton, and endowed in 1239. Walter de Merton, a Basingstoke man, became universally known as the founder of Merton College, Oxford. Later he was appointed Bishop of Rochester.

The 13th century saw a visit to Basingstoke by Henry III and in 1295 Basingstoke Borough Council returned two members to Parliament. In 1302 and 1306, the borough again returned two members to Parliament. In 1392 a serious fire broke out in the town and Richard III, in consideration of the great loss it occasioned, granted the inhabitants the rights of a corporation and the use of a common seal.

The town may not have been taxed as much as is the case today, but in 1250, King Henry III, having resolved to spend the festival of Christmas in his royal castle of Winchester, sent orders to various neighbouring towns to furnish provisions for the occasion. On the 30 November, a mandate was sent to the bailiffs of Basingstoke, commanding them to provide for the king's use two brawn hogs, to be sent to Winchester for the feast of the Nativity.

Another entry in an old document records an instance of an

unsuccessful execution at the gallows of the manor of Basingstoke. This was on 23 July 1261, when the sheriff was ordered to take bail for William le Neweman, confined in Winchester Prison, proved innocent of robbing the church of Steventon and of breaking from the prison of Basingstoke, for which he was due to be hanged. He escaped death when the cord on the gallows broke.

At a trial respecting the rights and privileges of the Crown, held at Winchester on the 15 February 1275, the third year of the reign of Edward I, the jury gave this verdict:

> That the men of Basingstoke have the return of writs and a gallows, assize of bread and beer, and other liberties which the lord King Henry, the father of the lord King who now is, granted to them by this charter. Also, that Walter de Merton has the assize of bread and beer in the town of Basingstoke (but the jury know not by what right) since the time the King delivered the said manor of Basingstoke.

At the end of the 15th century, Basingstoke had a visit from a famous foreign personage, Catherine of Aragon, who left Spain to live at Dogmersfield Palace. It is known that she spent a night in the home of Mr Kingsmill in Basingstoke. The purpose of her visit to England was to marry Prince Arthur, brother of Henry VIII. The ceremony took place in November 1501. Within two years, Prince Arthur, heir to the throne, died. Four years later she became King Henry VIII's first wife. Dogmersfield Palace was demolished many years ago and another house built on the site. The Basingstoke Canal runs through Dogmersfield.

ST MICHAEL'S CHURCH AND ALL SAINTS'

THE CURRENT Saint Michael's Church, the parish church of Basingstoke, provides a splendid example of Perpendicular architecture. Twice in its existence it has been ranked as a pro-cathedral, being the church of an archdeaconry.

It dates from the start of the 16th century, with the nave and aisles built 1510–21 and the church porch added in 1539. A priest's door was inserted on the north side of the chancel in 1525 and can be seen today, along with an entrance from the War Memorial Chapel, built in 1919 in memory of the many Basingstoke men who died in the 1914–18 conflict. Their names are recorded on the side of the north wall. The names of those who died in World War Two are in a book of remembrance.

The church once had a fine statue, probably of St Michael, which was removed by Lord Sandys in his official status on the orders of Thomas Cromwell in the 1530s and taken to London where, in all probability, it was smashed. Originally the church had two statues, one of St Thomas of Canterbury which occupied a portion of the north aisle, and one of the Blessed Virgin Mary in the south aisle. For many years St Stephen's Chapel has been to the south of the High Altar and this occupies what remains of the first church.

Many visitors are surprised to see the headpiece of the young Queen Victoria. This is a small bust gracing the chancel arch. It recalls the occasion when the Queen's father, the Duke of Kent, died at Sidmouth

Drawing of St Michael's Church, 1830.

The nave, St Michael's Church.

in 1820. His body was brought through Basingstoke on its way to burial at Windsor, and rested for a night at St Michael's Church. On the opposite side of the arch can be seen the head of Bishop Fox of Winchester, builder of the church.

Beneath the floor lie the remains of hundreds of former worshippers, and many more are buried in the churchyard.

The church has been exposed to great danger on several occasions. Once, during the Civil War, explosives stored in the church blew up, and in 1936 the ceiling over the south aisle was destroyed by fire while

Church Square before the bombing.

Demolition of the Methodist Church showing wooden surroundings, used partly to screen the demolition work.

Peals rung in St Michael's tower in 1890.

St Michael's Church seen through the trees.

Joint choirs festival at St Michael's Church.

the timbers were being treated for death-watch beetle. Chemicals were used and it is thought that a workman caused the blaze through smoking. A great amount of water was poured on the flames, which destroyed the church's magnificent three-manual organ.

To the regret of the organist and choristers, sufficient funds could not be found for another three-manual organ, and it was replaced by a two-manual instrument.

In the 19th century, church-going became more popular, and galleries were built on either side of the centre nave to increase the seating capacity to around a thousand. Sunday-school children normally used the galleries. They would aim little balls of paper at the adult congregation below, and as a result an extra verger had to be engaged to keep order.

Apparently the stanchions supporting the galleries were among the first goods brought to Basingstoke from Southampton following the opening of the new railway in 1840.

The worst disaster of all happened during a daylight bombing raid on 16 August 1940 when at about 5.30pm a stick of bombs fell on Church Square. One bomb narrowly missed the church. Nine people were killed in the raid. Another bomb fell between St

St Michael's Church choir, 1996.

Church Street, Basingstoke.

Michael's Church and the Methodist Church opposite, which was so badly damaged that it had to be rebuilt.

St Michael's Church lost all of its stained glass except for one window of Victorian glass.

Some years previously, mediaeval glass from the windows of the ruined Holy Ghost Chapel was fitted to the window at the north-east corner of St Michael's. When the War Memorial Chapel was built, the glass was moved to the exterior wall. It was reduced to many small fragments in the bomb blast. An anonymous man, realising the value of the glass, went round with a bag and collected what fragments he could. These were placed in a window on the south wall with some pieces large enough to be recognisable. Pieces of the Victorian glass were put in a window in the north wall opposite. All the stained glass which overlooked Church Street was pulverised, and the mullions of the windows were smashed. The damaged windows were beautifully restored, together with the windows on the south side.

One window, which had been dedicated to the memory of Mrs Kathleen Boustead, former Central President of the Mother's Union, who died in 1933, was among those destroyed. She was the wife of the

Laying the foundation stone of All Saints' Church, 1917. The architect was Temple Moore.

Former Popley curate Bill Ind after being consecrated bishop at St Paul's, where he is seen with Sister Charity. He is now Bishop of Truro.

then vicar, Canon Harry Boustead. One piece of glass retrieved bears the name 'Boustead'. The church was closed for several weeks while temporary repairs were effected.

Alterations have been made to the layout of the Church in recent years. A nave altar was introduced and the ornate wooden rood screen, placed to commemorate the Diamond Jubilee of Queen Victoria, was removed.

For many years, vicars of Basingstoke were scholars from Magdalen College, Oxford, with the eldest unmarried priest having the right to be appointed. The last Magdalen man to be appointed was Revd Simon Ridley in 1970. Since then, vicars have included Canon Nigel Harley, a Cambridge scholar, Canon Clifford Wright, educated at King's College, London and the present Team Rector, Revd Philip Welsh, a scholar of Keble College, Oxford.

For the past 25 years, Basingstoke has been a Team Ministry with a Team Rector and four Team Vicars.

St Michael's Church has a long choral tradition with one of the best parish church choirs in the diocese of Winchester. A feature of its ancient walls is a sundial. It also has a fine peal of eight bells and a very competent team of ringers, which has won several diocesan competitions in recent years.

All Saints' Church when completed.

Vicars of St Michael's Church

1244	Simon	1593	Ambrose Webb
1250	Sir Peter	1648	Stephen Evered
1277	Richard le Bel	1660	Richard White
1310	Sir Geoffrey Roc de Watesford	1685	Sir George Wheler
1310	Sir Vincent	1694	William Browne
1332	Sir John Tynctor	1697	John James
1332	Sir John Insular	1717	Umfrevile Fayrer
1343	Thomas de Babyngton	1723	Thomas Warton
1349	Thomas de Alton	1745	William Henchman
1351	John Chapelain de Basingstoke	1768	Thomas Sheppard
1361	Thomas Bourne	1814	James Blanch
1361	Sir John Carter	1864	James Elwin Millward
1398	Sir Edmund Weston	1891	H.R. Cooper Smith
1401	Sir Ralph Burgeys	1905	Harry W. Boustead
1447	John Howkyin	1936	Anthony W. Chute
1456	Master Henry Elwyke	1958	Norman J. Woodhall
1474	Master Thomas Raynys	1970	Simon Ridley
1499	Richard Gosmer	1973	Nigel Harley
1541	Edmund Kene	1981	Clifford Wright
1554	Sir Thomas Browne	1994	Philip Welsh
1587	Richard Eston		

The fact that four vicars were appointed between 1349 and 1361 reflects the death toll caused by the plague.

THE VYNE

THE VYNE, the beautiful Tudor mansion at Sherborne St John, three miles from Basingstoke, was built at the beginning of the 16th century by William Sandys, later Lord Sandys, a close friend of Henry VIII. The king visited The Vyne with his then queen, Anne Boleyn. It was said of Sandys that, throughout his long service to Henry VIII, he not only retained the king's confidence, 'but his head'. Henry made Sandys a Knight of the Bedchamber and gave him grants of land.

The Vyne, Sherborne St John.

Sandys was employed intermittently by the king overseas, and fought in Spain, Guyenne, Flanders and Picardy. In 1517 he was made Treasurer of Calais, in 1518 he became a Knight of the Garter and two years later he helped to organise the extravagant and famous ceremony of the Field of the Cloth of Gold. He was created Lord Sandys of the Vyne in 1523 and appointed Lord Chamberlain in 1526.

He was a great friend of Bishop Fox of Winchester, builder of St Michael's Church, Basingstoke and co-builder with Lord Sandys of the Chapel of the Holy Trinity adjoining the Holy Ghost Chapel. Both Lord and Lady Sandys were eventually buried at the chapel in a richly carved tomb.

Henry VIII gave Lord Sandys Mottisfont, near Romsey, in exchange for lands in Paddington and Chelsea, and Sandys eventually devoted all his interest to his new residence at Mottisfont.

Lord Sandys was succeeded by the 2nd Lord Sandys and then by a grandson William, 3rd Lord Sandys, who reigned at The Vyne for 67 years, entertaining Queen Elizabeth at the great house in 1569. Elizabeth made a second visit in 1601 when she was staying at Basing House. During the siege of Basing House in 1643, which resulted in the

Dining Room at The Vyne, 1999.

capitulation of the Royalists, Parliamentary troops under Sir William Waller were quartered at The Vyne.

Great changes were wrought to the house when it was purchased by a successful Middle Temple barrister, Chaloner Chute, in 1653. The Chute family were to remain at the house until 1956 with the death of Sir Charles Chute, who left The Vyne with its many acres of park and farmland to the National Trust.

The Vyne's grounds have been beautified by a lake which flows past the house. Actually it is the River Schirn, which rises at Sherborne St John and flows into the Loddon and, eventually, the Thames. Chaloner Chute built an immaculate portico which faces the lake. Many more changes occurred during John Chute's time at the house in the 18th century. John Chute was a close friend of Horace Walpole and the poet Gray. With the advice of his friends, great alterations were made to The Vyne. The traditional Tudor staircase was removed and replaced by one in the Corinthian and Doric style. It is so awe-inspiring that visitors can only stare at the beautiful architecture.

Other rooms with linenfold panelling remain, especially the Oak Gallery with over 400 panels, many depicting the arms of people associated with the house: Lord and Lady Sandys, Bishop Richard Fox, Sir Reginald Bray KG, Cardinal Wolsey and Catherine of Aragon. Complementing the carvings are a number of busts featuring Mary Queen of Scots, Shakespeare, Milton, Nero and Galba.

Another feature of this attractive house is the library, which houses many books assembled by W.L. Wiggett Chute. Perhaps the greatest

The Vyne hunt meeting leaving for the country on Boxing Day.

treasure of all is the chapel, described as one of the finest private chapels in England. The apsed bays of three late Gothic windows are filled with stained glass considered to be only equalled by the glass windows of King's College Chapel, Cambridge. The glass, which came from the Low Countries, was fashioned by men working in Basingstoke. It has long been believed that, during the time of the Civil War, the valuable glass was taken out and hidden in the murky waters of the lake.

Over 55,000 visitors a year, including many from overseas, visit this architectural and historical treasure on the doorstep of Basingstoke. In addition to the house, the extensive gardens and parkland are very popular with visitors.

The Saloon as it was at The Vyne as it was in 1999.

BASINGSTOKE IN THE 16TH CENTURY

I N THE 16th century Basingstoke took on a new look. The centre of the town changed dramatically, with St Michael's Church, with its grand tower, dominating the skyline. The church took several years to build during the opening years of the century. In 1540, Church Cottage, a marvellous Tudor building that is still in use today, was erected.

In the early days, Church Cottage contained a house for the vicar, but was later used as a tithe barn and a school. Its most attractive feature is the Chapter Room, and except for The Vyne, it has the best example of Tudor architecture in the area. The panelling sets off an open Tudor fireplace large enough to roast a pig.

The main hall, today known as the barn, was used to store wheat and other produce brought in from the fields at Winklebury as the vicar's

A drawing made in 1669 looking down on what is now Vyne Road to Basingstoke.

tithe. The room has fine timbers, some of which are thought to be former ships' timbers. An odd feature of the main hall is that excavations have shown that the hall was actually built over a tributary of the River

The Barn, Church Cottage, showing the Tudor beams.

Loddon, which over the years has washed away some of the foundations of the northern wall.

The schoolroom is so called because, during the closing years of the 19th century, a girls' school was held there. For many years a billiard table was at the west end of the hall, above which were Ten Commandments panels removed from above the chancel arch at St Michael's Church. Adjoining Church Cottage, on a footpath known as

Church Cottage, Church Square, built 1540.

Elbow Corner, is a Victorian annexe, known as the band room because the local town band at one time practised there. The band room is remarkable for its iron spiral staircase. An examination of the outer wall of Church Cottage can prove fruitful, for many of the bricks have notches cut in them, the result of scholars sharpening their slate pencils.

The 16th century also saw advances in education. Even before the building of the Holy Ghost Chapel at the Liten there was a Holy Ghost School, and part of that building is traced in the ruins of the Holy Ghost Chapel. Known as the Holy Ghost Guild, it was dissolved in 1550 by Edward VI and its land sold to John Dodington and William Warde. In 1556, Queen Mary restored the Holy Ghost Guild without its lands and constituted it a perpetual corporation.

It was then renamed Queen Mary's School, and later became Basingstoke Grammar School for boys, which until 1852 was centred in the old buildings by the Holy Ghost Chapel. It was a red letter day for Basingstoke when the school moved to new buildings in Worting Road, Basingstoke from where it was transferred in 1940 to another new site at the top of Vyne Road in the northern part of the town. With the reorganisation of secondary education in Basingstoke in 1972, Basingstoke Grammar School for boys was merged with the adjacent Charles Chute Secondary Modern School for boys to become The Vyne School. However, the newly established sixth form college, off Cliddesden Road, took the title of Queen Mary's College.

Among the scholars of the Basingstoke Grammar School were Gilbert White, author of *The Natural History of Selborne* and John Arlott, who was known the world over as a cricket commentator.

BURIED ALIVE

IN 1674 a circular reached many areas of Great Britain with the sensational headline 'News from the Grave'. The story was of a woman, Mrs Blunden, who had been buried alive in the Liten at Basingstoke.

If such an event was to happen today, with a buried woman shouting 'Take me out of the grave!' the news would steal the headlines of TV, radio and all the papers. The story, although seemingly incredible, is given credence by the fact that, at the Hampshire Assizes of 1675 – the Lent assizes – Basingstoke was fined the sum of £100. This was after a physician had stated on oath that after going through the usual procedure, he had been in no doubt that the lady had expired. Had the judge and jury not believed him, he and his associates who had given evidence would have paid with their lives.

Mr Blunden was a man of considerable reputation in Basingstoke as a maltster. He was married to a fat, gross woman who was very fond of her brandy. One evening, after her husband had left for London on business, she felt somewhat indisposed and sent her maid to the apothecary for a quantity of poppy water. Whether by the direction of a physician or by her own will, she drank so great a quantity of it that she fell into a deep sleep, insomuch that the people present concluded that she was dead, there being not the least palpitation of the heart,

Holy Ghost Church ruins.

motion of the pulses, breathing at her mouth or nose, nor any sensible warmth to be discerned in the whole body.

The apothecary was immediately sent for, and by surveying the remainder of the poppy water, gave a guess at what she had consumed and concluded she would not recover her senses in 48 hours at least, and therefore he supposed never. From these words of the apothecary they concluded her stark dead and that night laid her out, although one of the persons present observed that when she made any impression on the dead woman's face, the blood seemed to follow her finger. Either in haste or stupidity, little notice was taken of this observation.

Mrs Blunden's husband, who was on his way to London, was sent for and acquainted with the suddenness of the disaster. Having sudden and urgent business in London and considering his grief at home would do his wife no more good than at a distance, he continued on his journey. He would be able to buy mourning for himself and his family in London, and gave orders that the funeral should be deferred till his return, which he resolved should be on the Saturday after Tuesday 29 July, 1674.

His wife's relations, to whom the management of things was committed, began to consider that it was a great while to Saturday. The season of the year was hot, and the corpse fat – it would be impossible to keep her. They resolved to bury her the following day, which they did.

Many people, however, questioned that they would commit a person to the earth before they were fully satisfied she was dead, especially in her husband's absence and contrary to his order. However, it being none of their business, they offered nothing against, so that on the morrow, all things being ready for the funeral (but not the woman herself), they carried her to St Michael's Church. The coffin was set up on two stools (as the manner of the country was). One of the bearers perceived both the coffin and the stools to stir. He was so unseasonably merry that with a whisper to his neighbour, he told him that they had made Mrs Blunden's coffin so short that she could not be easy, for he plainly saw her stir. To which the other replied that if there were any motion it proceeded either from the weakness of the stools or the crowds of people that jogged them and so there was no further notice taken. At the end of the usual ceremonies, the coffin was placed on a bier and pulled up Chapel Street to the place of burial in the Liten and committed to the earth.

The following Friday, in the evening, some of the scholars of the town were at play in the churchyard near Mrs Blunden's grave, when they fancied they heard a kind of hollow voice, as if it were coming from underground. Listening more attentively they plainly heard somebody say 'Take me out of my grave'. The phrase was repeated several times and intermixed with fearful groans and dismal shriekings.

The boys were terrified and ran away and told several persons what

The Liten, as the Chapel Street cemetery has been known for years, with an 'x' marking the spot where Mrs Blunden was buried alive.

they had heard, but their story was so improbable that they were not believed. However, they stuck to their tale so steadfastly that on the next day, Saturday, the schoolmaster heard of it. He immediately reproved some and chastised others for relating such reports.

The boys, much incensed at their unjust correction, went again to Mrs Blunden's grave at midday on Saturday. Not without some fear, they laid their ears to the ground and heard the same words, if not so distinct yet with a louder voice. They went again and testified what they had formerly asserted.

The man they told was somewhat startled and began to consider some of the circumstances of her death and the funeral. He went to the grave and, by the direction of one of the boys, heard that what they said was true, although the voice seemed very faint and languishing.

He immediately tried to persuade the clerk to dig up the grave, but the clerk replied that he dared not do it without authority. By the time a minister and churchwardens could get together to consult about it, the afternoon was almost spent.

At last the grave was opened and when they opened the coffin, the corpse puffed up like a bladder. The joiner had made the coffin so short that they had had to press down upon her and keep her down with a stick while they nailed down the lid.

Now, surveying the body, they found it most lamentably beaten, and they concluded that the injuries had been a self-inflicted response to her confined circumstances. However, even with the most diligent scrutiny they could not detect any life remaining, and they let her down into the grave, intending to send for the coroner the following day. In the meantime, a watch was set to guard her during the night. The night was unseasonably wet, and it seems that her guards, having given up all hope of a second recovery, left her. In the morning, at their return to the grave, they found that she had torn off a great part of her winding sheet, scratched herself in several places and beaten her mouth until it bled.

This second neglect moved the hearts of all that heard of it, especially those who were concerned in the first discovery, and the coroner found in his judgement that her life had been clearly thrown away. He bound over several people concerned to answer charges at the next Assizes. They would have been indicted had not a physician of the town given it on oath that when the woman died, and was in her trance, he applied a looking glass to her mouth for a considerable time and could not discern the least breath to come from her. He had never failed with this test. All those called on to answer charges escaped with their lives, and the town of Basingstoke as a whole was fined for its neglect.

BASING HOUSE

THE MOST important siege of the Civil War took place at Old Basing, two miles from Basingstoke. Basing House, a Royalist stronghold and the home of the 5th Marquis of Winchester, withstood the onslaught of Cromwell's men for over two and a half years.

The house was built by Sir William Paulet, who was honoured by Henry VIII and acquired and left, it was said, greater wealth than any other subject since the Norman Conquest. He held the office of Lord Treasurer to the Household uninterruptedly through such diverse and stormy times as the reigns of Henry VIII, Edward VI, Mary and Elizabeth.

Basing House, which was much decayed, was rebuilt by him in the most sumptuous manner of his age and further great extensions were added by his successor. Sir William was created Marquis of Winchester while serving on the Council of Regency for Edward VI, and he was much esteemed by Queen Elizabeth. He died at the age of 87 in 1572. The Queen intimated that, had he been a younger man, she would have considered him as her consort. Royalty was often entertained at Basing House at great cost.

In July 1643 the Parliamentarian Colonel Norton, who had command of Hampshire troops at Southampton, was sent out with his forces into the country. Being too late to render assistance to Waller, he turned his attention to Basing. The marquis, for a defensive force, only had six musket-armed gentlemen. He repulsed Norton's initial attacks, as the rebel forces had no gunpowder or ladders to force an entry. The marquis appealed to the king after the loss of Reading, for 100 musketeers to reinforce his garrison, commanded by Lt.Col Peake. The Parliamentarian forces, 150 strong and commanded by Lord Hopton, were no match for the Royalist forces and in November had to retreat to their base at Farnham.

After the winter months curtailed any thought of again attacking the

Drawing of Old Basing house.

The ruins of Basing House.

house, in spring the Parliamentarians decided to starve out the garrison. From then on much fighting took place, and the fields around the house ran with blood from the 2,000 killed.

Skirmishes frequently happened in the park to the east of the house, and in the main street, where Royalists burned down most of the houses from which they were being sniped at from the bedrooms. The rebels used the church bells as a kind of alarm, until the peal was eventually removed by the Royalists. Another defensive position used by the Parliamentarians was Cowdery Down, the high ridge to the north of the house. This is where cavalry were mustered and shots fired on to the house by culverins and demi-culverins. Such early artillery were also mounted in the park not many yards from the great house.

From time to time, reinforcements were received by the garrison and often such added strength would see the Royalist soldiers venturing out to indulge in sallies, often along where the Basingstoke Canal was later built. These sallies reached as far as Basingstoke, where the Parliamentarians were billeted in St Michael's Church, which was also used as a store place for supplies, including ammunition, some of which exploded and damaged the church. Today, indentations in the stonework caused by musket fire can still be seen on the south walls of the church.

In some ways, the fighting could almost be described as gentlemanly, for often when prisoners were taken, representatives from the rebel forces would arrive at the entrance to the house seeking to exchange them for members of their own forces held prisoner within the strong walls.

On two occasions, efforts were made to persuade the Marquis of Winchester to surrender with the house and garrison. The first was on 11 July 1644 after Colonel Norton had been called away. With Herbert Morley in command, the following message was sent by drum:

> My Lord, to avoid the effusion of Christian blood, I have thought fit to send your Lordship this summon to demand Basing House to be delivered to me for the use of King and Parliament; if this be refused, the ensuing inconvenience will rest upon yourself, I desire your speedy answer, and rest, my Lord, Your Humble servant, Herbert Morley.

The marquis, after some deliberation, returned Mr Morley this answer:

> Sir, It is a crooked demand and shall receive its answer suitable. I keep the house in the right of my Sovereign, and will do it in despite of your forecast; your letter I will preserve as a testimony of your rebellion, Winchester.

This answer being returned by the drum with a 'Haste, haste post haste' on the letter, Lord Morley responded angrily by playing his guns for several days on the house's 'waterhouse'. At night, Coronet Bryan and some troopers, taking a message to Cowdrey's Down, brought in two prisoners.

On 2 September at noon, along with letters for the exchange of prisoners, the marquis received the following summons :

> My Lord, These are in the name and by the authority of the Parliament of England, the highest Court of Justice in the Kingdom, to demand the House and Garrison of Basing, to be delivered to me, to be disposed of according to order of Parliament. And hereof I expect your answer by this Drum within one hour, after the receipt hereof, in the mean time, I rest, Yours to serve you, Rich Norton'.

To which the Lord Marquis instantly despatched this answer:

> Sir, Whereas you demand the House and Garrison of Basing by a pretended authority of Parliament, I make this answer,

Basing ruins.

that, without the King, there can be no Parliament, by His Majesty's commission I keep the place, and without His absolute command, shall not deliver it to any pretenders whatsoever. I am, yours to serve you, Winchester.

This answer sent, the opposing forces let fly from their new battery by the town. In six hours they thundered six-score shot by cannon and culvering, and they destroyed one of the great brick towers from which the garrison had targeted their attackers. They killed three of the garrison, and hurt a woman.

Exchanges of prisoners continued while fighting intensified throughout 1644 and 1645, and the Parliamentarian forces drawn up in the vicinity of the house numbered thousands instead of hundreds. In September 1645, after Fairfax had taken Bristol, Cromwell was dispatched with a brigade of three regiments of foot and three of horse, for the taking of certain Royalist garrisons. Basing was chief among them.

Cromwell himself arrived in Basingstoke to supervise the final overthrow of Basing House. The onslaught started at 6am on 14 October 1645. Cromwell was lodged in the Fleur de Lys, an old inn which stood on the spot close to where the Basingstoke post office stands today in London Street. The overcoming of the garrison by far superior forces was completed in two hours. Although the garrison fought courageously, 74 were killed, some after capture. Many saved their lives by disclosing treasure to their captors. The marquis was discovered hiding in an oven and was taken away to be held a prisoner in the Bell Inn, London Street, opposite Cromwell's quarters.

The marquis was dealt with as a gallant enemy and eventually went to France. The plunder from the house was valued at the enormous sum, for those days, of £200,000. Included were jewels and treasure worth £50,000, richly decorated furniture and hangings, including a bed with its furniture worth £1,300. At night, a furious fire, caused by neglect in quenching a fireball, consumed all that was left.

Among the prisoners were the Deputy-Governor Sir Robert Peake, a bookseller at Holborn Bridge, Inigo Jones the architect and two famous engravers, Hollar and Fairthorne. Those who fell during the siege were Dr Thomas Johnson the botanist and Major Cuffaud, a member of a family who lived at a historic house at Cuffaud Lane, near Bramley, claiming cousinship with the Plantagenets and Tudors.

MUNICIPAL LIFE AND CHARTERS

SOME OF Basingstoke's municipal records have been destroyed by fires, notably the great blaze of 1392 and another in the 20th century. The latter destroyed some records held at the Muniments Room at the civic offices. During Queen Elizabeth's visit to Basingstoke in 1601 the town was again the victim of fire. Many thatched buildings were destroyed. The queen, who was staying at Old Basing, was so concerned that she was the main instigator in begging assistance from neighbouring counties, one of which was as far away as Devonshire.

One of the earliest references to municipal government was made by William, the provost from 1205 onwards, who was required to supply 10 armed men for the king's service in 1212. The county quota for soldiers was fixed at 40 from Winchester, 20 from Southampton, 10 from Alton and 10 from Basingstoke. It would appear, however, that the corporate life of the borough commenced with the charter of Henry III in 1227, which granted the manor at a rent of £72 12s. In 1256 another charter assessed the rent at £80, which was later confirmed by Edward III in 1329, Henry V in 1414 and Henry VI in 1449. With this last the privilege of a Whitsuntide Fair was added.

In 1622 a charter of James I appointed two bailiffs and 14 chief burgesses, and one issued by Charles I in 1641 appointed a mayor, seven aldermen and 12 councillors. Aldermen remained until the reorganisation of local government in 1972 when, for a time, the council was headed by a chairman working alongside a town mayor. This arrangement was quickly amended, and a mayor was appointed annually for the borough of Basingstoke and Deane. This area stretches from Brown Candover in the south to the Berkshire border in the north, in the east to a short distance from Old Basing and to the west almost to the borders of Andover. The area includes such large villages as Old Basing, Tadley and district, Oakley, Overton and Whitchurch.

From early times, the administration of justice was in the hands of two bailiffs, elected by the freeholders of the town. They presided over the courts of the hundred and the half-yearly views of 'frank pledge', at which all the freeholders had to report themselves. The court records show that these courts exercised jurisdiction in resisting encroachment, enforcing trade regulations and abating nuisances.

The most common offences under the court laws were for 'breaking the assize', that was, overcharging for ale and bread. Often the fine was ninepence. Other common offences were leaving gutters and ditches uncleansed and depositing waste matter to block roads and pavements. There are instances of common assault recorded such as that of Johanna, who drew blood from Isabella, and Isabella, who drew blood from Jonathan. Each was fined 6d. Even John the Rector made an assault on a certain Thomas, using a stick and also drawing blood. For both these counts he was fined 6d.

Poaching was an offence which was often dealt with and there is a case of William Rooke, keeper of Privett Park (Park Prewett) who was twice fined 12d for poaching on the king's preserves. William Rooke bequeathed his name to posterity as the west end of Park Prewett, where Saxonwood is today, is still known as Rook's Down.

In mediaeval times, Basingstoke was little more than a large village. Water came from the many wells, the streets were unpaved and unlit and there was no sewerage system. For some years, the sewage ran into the River Loddon. In an age when there was little transport linking one town to another, Basingstoke had to be self-supporting. Apart from those in business as butcher, baker and dairyman, a list drawn up in 1464 included the brazier, brewer, tapster, half-tapster, chandler, tanner, currier, joiner, arrow maker, saddler, haberdasher, hosier, dubber of cloth and half-dubber, miller, cooper, dyer, and tiler.

Manufacture of cloth was of such special importance. As many as 30 broadcloths and 100 kersies were made in Basingstoke. Output had fallen by the 17th century because of opposition coming from clothmakers at Reading and Newbury. A damaging report to the Basingstoke manufacturers was that the cloth made by those in neighbouring towns was 'more falsely made than white cloth ever was'. History seems to have repeated itself with Mr Burberry setting up his first workshop in Basingstoke and patenting his remarkable waterproof gaberdine. The early cloth trade had practically died out by 1786.

CHURCH REGISTERS

CHURCH registers are most useful sources of information about the history of town or country areas. Of equal value are churchwarden's accounts, which at St Michael's in Basingstoke date back to 1621, some 18 years before the first parish register. The accounts also record the yearly payments for ringing the church bells on the monarch's coronation day and birthday, on 5 November to commemorate the Gunpowder Plot, and on other occasional days when the ringers commanded additional payments.

It is surprising how many instances there are of royalty passing through the borough. James I passed through the town in 1623, followed by Queen Henrietta Maria in 1626 and Queen Katherine of Braganza in 1662. In 1671, Charles II came to Basingstoke. James II passed through the town in 1683 and again in 1688, only five weeks before his flight to France. William III came through the town in 1693 and on 28 August George I visited the town to stay at Hackwood House as the guest of the Duke of Bolton. To commemorate his visit, he presented a statue of himself on his horse, which was mounted on a pedestal outside Hackwood House. The accounts show how much was paid to the bell ringers on these royal occasions. When James I passed through the town, the bell ringers received 12p and the insertion gives details of the occasion:

> ...the King left Whitehall on Monday, July 21st, 1623. On the following day he dined at Hartford Bridge on his way to Basing and ate fruit sent from Bramshill. The King slept at Basing House on Tuesday night and on the Wednesday he passed through Basingstoke on his way to Andover.

Apart from bell-ringing for royal occasions, knells were rung when parishioners were buried and this was another important source of income for the church. So too was the money paid for the privilege of having one's own seat in church. The burgesses, aldermen and even the mayor, on their appointment to the council, had to pay a shilling each for their respective seats. A similar sum was paid by their ladies to sit in the burgesses' wives' seats. This was a proud distinction and an envied privilege. The amounts paid for wives' seats varied according to the position of the pews, ranging from four pence to as much as three shillings for the special pews.

In 1662 a Mrs Juliana Hatfield gave a pulpit cloth of green velvet to the church with the request that whenever it was used at a funeral, 12 pence should be paid and the money distributed among the poor. This benefaction brought in many shillings which were doled out to the recipients on funeral days. The custom continued until 1645 when the pulpit cloth appears to have been stolen by Parliamentary soldiers, along with the silver communion cup and cover and other articles belonging to the church. At the time, Parliamentary soldiers were billeted in the church.

Also in 1662, the first gallery was built and repairs were made to the church, which the parishioners were asked to help finance. The amount of £48 16s 5d was raised, a considerable sum in the 17th century.

During the siege of Basing House, there were many records made in the accounts of skirmishes in Basingstoke. In 1643 there is an entry:

> paid for digging 21 graves, 7 shillings and for carrying six
> men and digging their graves, 8 shillings. Richard Beckley
> (beadle) for digging five graves 1s 8d. For digging the grave
> in the churchyard, 6d, and for carrying two men and digging
> their graves 1s 8d. Paid Richard Beckley for making clean the
> church, 1s 10d.

Some of the graves would have been dug beneath the floor of the church. During the 1990s, when new heating was being installed in the church, workmen broke through the floor into a domed shape canopy, exposing two skeletons. Also, when the new nave altar area was being made and tiles laid, one tile would not lie level. It was found that the side of a child's coffin had risen to the surface.

When the excavations were being made in 1920 for the building of the War Memorial Chapel, graves were exposed and rings were taken from the fingers of the skeletons within. On hearing of the thefts, the vicar, Canon Boustead, went into town that evening and took several rings from the workmen drinking in the town's pubs.

The churchwarden's accounts show that material from the ruins of Basing House was brought to St Michael's following the order for the demolition of Basing House '…that whoever fetches away the materials shall have them for their pains'. This insertion follows: 'Paid Thomas Arnold for taking down 4,000 tiles at Basing, 10s, and for two days work for his man to help load tiles at Basing, 20d'.

All sorts of repairs had to be undertaken to the woodwork, pews, windows and doors of the church. Help was given nationally and in 1647 there is this entry:

> …paid for the charges of Mr Webb (the Vicar), Mr Stocker and William Clough for their journey to London to the Company of Skinners for the getting of our money due to the town from them, with other charges in London about the same business, 46s.

The church accounts refer to the plague breaking out in Basingstoke. In 1666, one year after the plague hit London, there were upwards of 80 knells recorded at St Michael's Church. In 1671, John Edwards and his men were paid 6s 8d for taking down St Michael's bells and loading them to be taken to Reading for re-casting. When Mr John Knight, the bell founder, visited the church he was paid £50 4s 0d for carting two bells and providing one new bell.

OLD BASINGSTOKE

THE GUNPOWDER Plot of 1605 was commemorated in Basingstoke by an elm tree planted almost opposite Sir James Deane's Almshouses in London Street. The tree, which grew very large, almost blocked the end of London Street by the crossroads. The tree was cut down in 1809 by a local tradesman who said he would make no charge if he could have the timber. The girth of the tree was 14 feet. The man who offered to do the work lost out, for the tree was rotten inside and only fit for firewood.

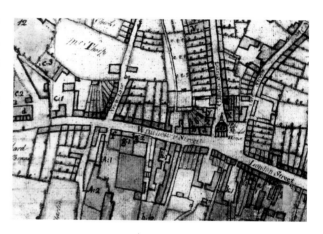

A map of the main street of Basingstoke in 1750.

A general description of the town, found in Philemon Holland's 1937 translation of Camden's *Britannia*, describes Basingstoke as 'a mercate towne well frequented upon the descent of an hill'. The town lies in the hollow between two hills. From that on the north, where the Holy Ghost Chapel stands, the road passed along what was in 1557 named Hollie Ghost Street, otherwise known as Whiteways (now Chapel Street) to the foot of Church Street. At this point there was the 'causey' (causeway), for the repair of which Sir James Deane in 1607 left 20 shillings a year. In April 1884, during the repairs of the main drain in Church Street, a number of oak piles were discovered, about five feet apart, which appear to have carried a footbridge over what was, at one time, a watercourse.

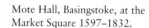

Mote Hall, Basingstoke, at the Market Square 1597–1832.

The River Loddon has always been important for Basingstoke, and the waterway was referred to as 'the sweet native stream' by Thomas Warton the Younger. Some evidence of the river's significance is found in street names. We have Lower Brook Street and Brook Street, and at one time there was a

View of Basingstoke from the Chapel Hill cemetery in 1857.

A drawing showing when Basingstoke pig market was outside Sir James Deane's almshouse, London Street.

North Brook Street where the tunnel takes what is now named Churchill Way under the town centre. There were in fact two River Loddons, the Little Loddon, rising near the junction of Flaxfield Road and Sarum Hill, which meets with the main River Loddon in Glebe Gardens, and the main river itself.

The name 'Flaxfield' or 'Flaxpool' is generally supposed to bear witness to futile legislation introduced by Henry VIII, which attempted to enforce the cultivation of flax by Act of Parliament. The prescribed amount of flax to be produced was in the proportion of one rood to every threescore acres of land. At the time of the Napoleonic Wars, a barn was used in Flaxfield to house French prisoners of war. Others were held at Odiham in the ancient chalk-pit, from where they were kept within bounds, one being the 'Frenchman's Oak', about a mile away from the chalk-pit.

The attempt to cultivate flax by a state order was not successful. An attempt was made during the reign of Queen Elizabeth I to popularise silk production.

There is a large coat of arms dated 1597 in St Michael's Church which was given to Basingstoke for the support given to the silk

industry. Not far from the church was the silk mill and nearby, in Glebe Gardens, can be seen a mulberry tree.

In the 18th century it was the woollen industry which was encouraged. All those who died had to be buried wearing woollen cloth, and this was recorded in the parish registers, which can be seen at the County Records Office, Winchester. In one of the registers there is a record of the Earl of Portsmouth being fined £100 for failing to bury a relative in woollen clothing.

In Baigent and Millard's *History of Basingstoke* of 1889, reference is made to the change and decay that rapidly removed the few lingering relics of old Basingstoke street architecture. It is recorded that:

> a half-timbered house, with projecting upper storey and 'herring-bone' work in brick, stands near the church in Elbow Corner. It is Vicarial property, and was probably the old Vicarage House. The lower room is large, with panelled walls and a low ceiling, supported by massive beams. A house over-hanging the Loddon, in Church Street, retains a highly ornamented brick gable of good design, which is perhaps as early as the time of James I. One or two houses in Church

Sir James Deane's almshouses, built 1608.

Basingstoke Market Place, 1850.

Olde worlde Basingstoke –
thatched cottages in Hackwood
Road.

Street also contain panelling more or less richly carved, some of which, however, has been imported.

It is further recorded that:

a corner-house between Cross Street and Church Street, till lately contained some panelling of the time of Queen Elizabeth, with a shield bearing the arms of the Puttenham family, quartering those of the Warblington family. These were probably relics from the town residences of the Warblingtons, lords of Sherfield-on-Loddon, who held in Basingstoke a messuage and garden, with sixty acres of arable land and four acres of meadow. William Puttenham, married one of the heiresses of the Warblington family, and his descendants inherited thereby the manor of Sherfield-on-Loddon. The coat of arms was probably put up in the time of Sir George Puttenham.

The tokens used by navvies excavating the Basingstoke Canal are well known and can be seen in the Willis Museum. Tradesmen's tokens, issued in the place of copper coins during the second half of the 17th century, are much more scarce. They give some idea of the conditions of trade in Basingstoke in that period. Only ten of the tokens have survived. The earliest is that of John Coleman the elder, dated 1652, the reverse of which bears a bird in the centre. He was churchwarden in 1670 and his name appears on the tenor bell of St Michael's Church. His co-churchwarden, Henry Barfoot, issued in 1669 a token bearing a lion rampant. George White, probably a druggist,

Old cottages in Chapel Street.

has a pestle and mortar as his badge. George White was the son of Hugh White of Basingstoke, an apothecary. According to the parish registers, he was baptised on 8 August 1640 and buried on 28 December 1676.

Samuel Kitchener's calling was displayed on his token, which bears the tallow-chandlers' arms. Another of the same craft, John Watts junior, exhibits a man making candles. A further token has the name of John Trimmer and is dated 1670. Barnard Reve (or Ryve) issued more than one token, marked with an angel. He was warden of the Holy Ghost Guild in 1645 and again in 1653, was proprietor of the Angel Inn, which was probably named after the patron saint of the town, St Michael. The token of John Masefield, dated 1669, is not circular as was usual, but heart-shaped. The token of Robert Blunden bears the device of a rabbit.

One of Basingstoke's famous inns of the past, part of the high building which can still be seen in Winchester Street, was the Maidenhead Inn. This was where, on 14 August 1686, Sir Henry St George, Clarencieux King at Arms, with his pursuivants and attendants, held his court for the purpose of registering the pedigrees of the neighbouring gentry. This was the last Heraldic Visitation held by the officials of the College of Arms in England. In 1802, an advertisement in the *Hampshire Chronicle* designated it 'The Bolton Arms Inn, late the Maidenhead Inn'.

Basingstoke had two racecourses, one at the old Down, Kempshott, and the other on Basingstoke Common on what is now the Black Dam estate. The paper called the *Post Boy* of 16 July 1713 advertises:

A plate to be run for, on Basingstoke Down, on August 3rd, 1713, of about £10 value, by any horse, mare or gelding, 14

A peep back into Victorian days. The Ship Inn, Market Square.

Blacksmith's at Silchester, 1890. Apart from the 'modern' bicycle, this scene is typical of blacksmith's shops duriong the preceding centuries.

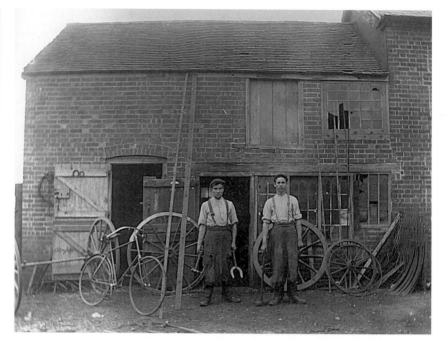

hands, to carry 10 stone and to all even pounds to an inch, be it more or less, and to be shown at the George Inn, Basingstoke, the Monday before, between the hours of 10 and 12, the winning horse to be sold for £10.

A very handsome silver punch-bowl was preserved at The Vyne, inscribed 'Basingstoke Plate, October 2nd, 1688'. It was believed to have been won at the races on Basingstoke Down by Mr Edward Chute, grandson of the Speaker, Chaloner Chute.

Basingstoke's other racecourse traversed the top of the Little Common and was in use during the Napoleonic Wars. According to the Basingstoke Common minute book, the racing authorities only applied for the use of the common three days before a meeting was held. Permission was given but certain restrictions were imposed as meetings were held on Sundays. The Horse and Jockey Inn, which stood in Hackwood Road, was so named because of the close proximity of the racecourse.

NAMES

LOCAL names of people, streets, roads and their derivations are a matter of local interest and they reveal much about the history of the town. One of the best known names in Basingstoke is that given to the town's museum – the Willis Museum. Until a few years ago, the Willis Museum was situated in New Street, but when plans to convert the Town Hall into commercial premises were abandoned, the museum was relocated there.

The name of Willis goes back to the 19th century to a jeweller's shop which was originally in Church Street but moved to Wote Street. A reconstruction of the façade of this shop is to be found as part of a street scene in the Milestones Museum.

George Willis was a watch and clock maker but his name lives on for the part he played in civic affairs and the contribution he made to researching the history of his birthplace. He also unearthed various geological finds in the area. With his friend Horace Carey, a Basingstoke tailor, he spent many hours searching for fossils and many of their finds are on display in the Willis Museum. He became mayor of Basingstoke in the 1920s, and after the end of World War Two was honoured by the town when he was made the first Freeman of Basingstoke. He made a great contribution to the town as a member of the borough council and he was a magistrate and school governor. Horace Carey had his tailoring business in Church Street and was one of the private retailers who made a real contribution to the business life of the town before the days of town development.

Winchester Street and London Street formed part of the A30 road and were originally to be called the High Street. As it was the main thoroughfare along which the stage coaches regularly passed on the way from Winchester to London, long before the days of the railway, the two names were automatically fixed in the minds of townsfolk.

A feature of the town's estates is the relation they have to a general theme. The Buckskin estate, which separates Basingstoke from Worting, has roads and footpaths named after mountains. As the extensive development at Kempshott grew, the roads there were named after birds and flowers.

The roads on the Berg private estate, which separates the South Ham area from Kempshott, bear the names of mayors of the 17th century, including Richard Brackley, Edmund Pitman and Richard Woodroffe, and mayors of the 18th century, John Abbott and Samuel Shipton. Other mayors of that period, such as Giles Lyford and George Baynard, have roads named after them on the South View estate.

Great care has to be taken when designating names for new roads in order to avoid duplication and confusion. For example, the roads on the Riverdene estate in Basingstoke bear the names of rivers, hence its name. However, a few miles away at East Oakley there are also roads named after rivers.

When the extension to the South Ham estate was completed in the 1960s, a novel idea was to name the roads after those who had died in World War Two. The names were taken from those on the War Memorial in the Memorial Park and include Alliston, Burnaby, Butler and Dibley.

The Harrow Way estate to the south of the town is so called because of the estate's close proximity to the Harrow Way, which was used by pilgrims visiting the tomb of Thomas Becket in Canterbury Cathedral. The roads on this estate include the names of former masters of the Holy Ghost School in the Liten. Merriat Close is named after Richard Merriat, who was rector of Dummer before taking up his post as master in January 1606. Morley Close is named after the Rt Revd George Morley, Bishop of Winchester, a distinguished promoter of learning, who in 1670 re-opened the Holy Ghost School after it had been closed for a number of years. Loggon Road is named after Samuel Loggon, who was appointed Master in 1743 and later became rector of Stratfield Turgis. He is particularly remembered for drawing up a petition in which particulars were stated about the state of the buildings and property of the school and concerning a right of patronage dispute. Lightfoot Close is named after William Barber Lightfoot, who was appointed Master in the 19th century. The main road through the Harrow Way estate is Sheppard Road, named after Thomas Sheppard, a Fellow of Magdalen College, Oxford. He was instituted as vicar of Basingstoke in 1768 and became one of the town's benefactors.

Kingsmill is the name of a famous local family and the name is commemorated on the Harrow Way estate. It was in the house of Mr Kingsmill that Catherine of Aragon slept in November 1509, the night before she left for Dogmersfield Palace where she became betrothed to Prince Arthur. After his premature death, she became the first wife of Henry VIII.

The Warton family, of which Thomas senior was a vicar and Thomas junior the Poet Laureate, are honoured by Warton Road, in South View. Dr James Millard, co-author of Baigent and Millard's *History of Basingstoke*, is commemorated with a road named after him on the Oakridge estate.

Roads named after mayors of the 20th century include Hillary Road at Oakridge and Chesterfield Road on the Hackwood Road estate. Roads named after councillors of that period include Howard Road and Pheby Close.

Sarum Hill, named after the original name of Salisbury, was formerly known as Salisbury Road. The names of roads in the Essex Road area were built by an Essex builder and were named after towns in Essex such as Rayleigh, Rochford and Southend. These roads now form part of the Brookvale area.

Two of Basingstoke's outstanding sons have been honoured by having roads named after them on the first local authority housing estate to be built in the town. Walter de Merton was founder of Merton College, Oxford and Sir James Lancaster was the founder of the East India Company.

The roads and closes of Basingstoke's very large Brighton Hill area have been given the names of famous composers, ranging from Bach to Sullivan and Gershwin to Ketelbey. The Black Dam estate roads and closes are named after painters such as Gainsborough, Holbein, Renoir and Van Dyck.

The names of the roads and closes on the Popley estates are named after abbeys, islands and poets. The older part of South Ham estate honours Lord Sandys, builder of The Vyne, and Lord Bolton, who was associated with Hackwood Park for many years. Lord Camrose, the last owner of Hackwood House, is also honoured, with Camrose Way situated near to his former estate.

In Basingstoke town centre, one road created after the 1960s development, Timberlake Road, is named after a famous man who was educated at Fairfields School, namely Tim Timberlake. His father owned a jeweller's shop in Wote Street and when Tim was a teenager, the family emigrated to Canada. Tim moved to the United States and was very successful in Los Angeles where he became head of the council. The naming of the road occurred after he returned for a short stay in Basingstoke, where he was given a civic reception.

JOHN WESLEY

ONE OF the great religious leaders to visit Basingstoke was John Wesley, who led the Methodist revival and in so doing visited the town on more than one occasion during the 18th century. The following notes were mostly taken from *The Journals of John Wesley*, written by Mr G.B. Mellor, a Wesleyan minister at Southsea.

A letter from Revd Thomas Warton, vicar of Basingstoke from 1723 to 1745, addressed to the Town Clerk of Basingstoke, Mr John Russell, attorney at law, is still preserved in manuscript form, dated 13 February 1738. It reads as follows:

> They wrote from Basingstoke, that on Sunday last the Reverend Mr Charles Kinchin, MA, Rector of the Church of Dummer in the Bishop of Winchester's Diocese, and Fellow of Corpus Christi (where his Lordship is Visitor) held a publick meeting consisting chiefly of Dissenters of both sexes, who were very numerous, at the Crown Inn in that Town, where he prayed much extempore and expounded or preached after the manner of the Methodists, taking a whole chapter for his text; the noted Mr Whitfield (an itinerant preacher lately arrived from Georgia) having done the same at the King's Head on the Thursday, and at the Crown on the Friday and Saturday next preceding. NB: It is presumed that the aforesaid Inns have license to sell ale and other liquors usually retailed at Publick Houses, but for no other purpose whatsoever.

John Wesley also made repeated visits to

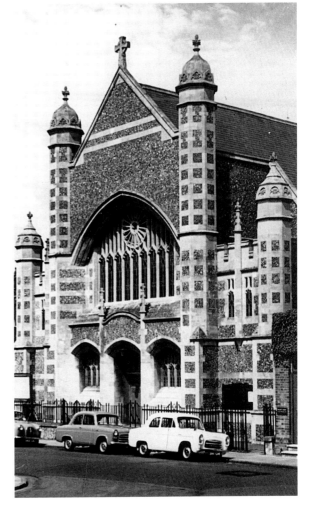

Methodist Church, Church Street.

Basingstoke for the purpose of preaching between the years 1739 and 1763, as the following extracts from his journals reveal:

March 10th, 1739, Saturday. In the afternoon I came to Dummer, and on Sunday morning had a large and intelligent congregation. I was desired to expound in the evening at Basingstoke.

April 29th. Expounded to a small company in the evening at Basingstoke. December, 1747. Passed through Basingstoke.

October, 1751. We rode leisurely on to Basingstoke and came about two hours after sunset to Bramsel (Bramshill).

February 10th, 1759. Rode to Basingstoke, where the people put me in mind of the wild beasts at Ephesus. Yet they were unusually attentive in the evening.

Saturday, 13th, 1759. After preaching to a small serious company, I went on to London.

September 24th, 1759. Preached at 8am at Brentford, and in the evening at Basingstoke, to a people slow of heart and dull of understanding.

November, 1759, Friday, 26th. I rode to Basingstoke, was extremely tired, when I first came in, but much less so afterwards.

Monday, November 3rd, 1760. Preached at 9am at Andover to a few dead stones, at 1pm in Whitchurch, and in the evening at Basingstoke.

1763, Friday, September 30th. From Whitchurch to Basingstoke. Even here there is at length some prospect of doing good. A large number of people attended, to whom God enabled me to speak strong words, and they seemed into the hearts of the hearers.

1763, Saturday, 25th October. Preached at Basingstoke, where many attended at five in the morning. In the afternoon I came to London.

The parish register records under the date of 22 November 1736 'Elizabeth Box, widow of Edward Box, was buried in woollen'. The following is therefore of interest. The semi-political High Churchmanship of Queen Anne's days, which culminated in the extravagant popularity of Dr Sacheverell, had at least one representative in Basingstoke. The following obituary notice was quoted by the

Atheneum in 1874 from the *Grub Street Journal* of Thursday 23 December 1736.

> Basingstoke, December 9th. This day was interred in our churchyard Dame Box, a zealous woman for the Church. When Dr Sacheverell was cleared from his troubles, she clothed her self in white, and kept the same clothes by her, and was buried in them. During the Doctor's life she constantly went to London once a year, and carried with her a dozen larks as a present to that High-flying priest. Her corpse was adorned with oaken boughs in memory of King Charles II.

The 'Primitive Methodists had no regular footing in Basingstoke before 1833, when Mr Edward Bishop, one of their ministers, preached in the open-air at Totterdown (the area at the bottom of Reading Road where the Steam Dell was), amid much opposition. The use of a court in Bunnian Place was afterwards allowed to their preachers, the hearers standing in the road. Services were then held in a timber-yard lent by Mr Etheridge. It was not until 1847 that the Primitive Methodists had a small chapel built in Flaxfield, which was enlarged in 1863 and again in 1881. It was then that the Primitive Methodists had a resident minister and 30 local preachers.

CHUTE HOUSE

A BUILDING very much connected with Basingstoke's history is Chute House, situated in Glebe Gardens at the bottom of Church Street. It is a Georgian building, erected nearly 300 years ago, and served as Basingstoke's rectory until the late 1960s, when a new but much smaller rectory was built. The old rectory then became the headquarters of the Basingstoke council for community service.

Chute House is named after the Venerable Archdeacon Chute, brother of Sir Charles Chute of The Vyne. An aristocrat and a bachelor, he turned the rectory into a clergy house where his four curates lived, among them some who later became well-known clerics. The curate he brought with him from Highfield, Southampton was the Revd George Addleshaw, who was given charge of All Saints' Church. When he moved on, it was to become principal of St Chad's College, Durham, from where he was appointed a residential canon of York Minster and treasurer of the Cathedral. He subsequently moved from York on his appointment as dean of Chester Cathedral. As a writer, he wrote a book on the rituals of the Church of England. Another curate who lived at the rectory was the Revd Christopher Campling, who became dean of Ripon Cathedral.

In the days when Chute House was a clergy house, the Venerable Archdeacon Chute worked his curates hard. In addition to their ministry, in the summer months they were required to take a scythe and cut the long grass which grew in the vicar's meadow. Seventy-five years ago, the incumbent of Basingstoke employed a cook, housemaid, parlour maid, chauffeur and gardener, who combined the post with that of being a verger.

The Warton family, all poets, lived at the old rectory. Thomas Warton Junior was born there on 9 January 1728. By the time he was 25, he had written most of his poems, which resulted in him becoming Poet Laureate in 1785. His most famous works were *The Pleasures of Melancholy* and *The History of English Poetry*.

Set in an oasis of quiet, the River Loddon runs through the grounds of Glebe Gardens and passes by what was once a beautiful lawn where the rectory Garden Fête was held annually at midsummer. This ceased when the new rectory was built and where the lawn once was there are now many trees. When Canon Harry Boustead, a keen rower who had rowed in the Magdalen College eight, was vicar, he had his old oar stretched diagonally across a wall of one of the rooms in the rectory. He also had a punt which he allowed his choirboys to propel alongside the lawn, the river being much wider than it is today.

A task set for choirboys when showery rain threatened was to raise the sluice gates to save the lawn from flooding. The river flows under the road through a culvert where Coppyn Bridge used to be. In the 1970s, Chute House was severely damaged by fire but the building was rebuilt.

As a boy, I knew Canon Boustead well. He was a doctor of divinity, and a lovely man, but during the first years he was in Basingstoke, he was very bigoted about the chapels and this led him to make the front page of the national papers. When the mayor, Mr Cannon, a London Street butcher, was his churchwarden, he told the vicar that he would be attending St Michael's Church for the morning civic service, but would be attending the evening service at the Congregational Church. Canon Boustead refused to allow this and told the mayor that if he pursued his course the doors of St Michael's Church would be barred to him for the mayoral service. In the event that is what happened. The canon relented in later years and took much interest in the chapter for all the clergy of the town.

Canon Norman Woodhall was the last incumbent to live at Chute House, which was much too capacious. He moved to a smaller house in Bounty Road when it was decided to build a new, smaller rectory in what was part of the Glebe Gardens. These gardens are a haven of beauty in the middle of a busy town where, in springtime, the snowdrops and daffodils make a picturesque scene. The Borough of Basingstoke and Deane takes a close interest in Glebe Gardens, which the borough staff maintain exceedingly well.

Glebe Gardens, in clement weather, is a favourite spot for many office and shop workers, who can be seen eating their packed lunches.

The gardens are still used by the young peoples' organisations which use Church Cottage as their headquarters. A small part of the gardens is used as a car park for business people and shoppers during the daytime and for the patrons of the Anvil Concert Hall in the evening. The Glebe has been used as a pleasant spot for hundreds of years. At one time there were trout to be seen in the River Loddon.

On the opposite side of Brook Street, which adjoins Glebe Gardens, May's Brewery stood for 200 years. With the wind in the right direction, Glebe Gardens would be filled with the aroma of hops. Adjoining the gardens was the Silk Mill, and it is interesting to note that a mulberry tree, the leaves of which were used to feed silkworms, is still to be found in the Glebe.

JANE AUSTEN

THE MOST famous person of the North Hampshire area is undoubtedly the writer Jane Austen, born in the small hamlet of Steventon in 1775, the daughter of the rector. Jane lived at Steventon until moving to Bath in 1801.

Travellers from Basingstoke to Overton pass the turning to Steventon, where an olde worlde inn called Deane Gate stands. Steventon is a backwater of Hampshire and to reach it one has to pass through a tunnel beneath the Basingstoke to Winchester railway, which was built on a high embankment.

St Nicholas's Church, Steventon, Jane Austen's birthplace.

The Oakley Post Office in the village that was so well known to Jane Austen.

Steventon Church, where Jane must have worshipped countless times, remains unspoilt. It is a very pleasant spot, away from the noise of traffic. During the 25 years Jane lived in the village, she enjoyed what life had to offer and was well known at the large houses where she had many friends. Jane knew Basingstoke very well, and attended dances at the Assembly Rooms, little better than stables, which stood to the rear of what is now Barclays Bank, just off the Market Place. She also dined at the Crown Inn on Winchester Street, with the courtyard off Windover Street, an inn well-known to the Prince Regent when he stayed at Kempshott House, his hunting lodge.

It was during one of her visits to the home of Mr Bigg-Wither, not far from Deane Gate, where Jane experienced her first romance with the young Mr Bigg-Wither. During the evening they actually became engaged to be married, but alas! it was one of the shortest engagements ever, for Jane had second thoughts and broke it off the next morning.

It was at Steventon that Jane wrote a number of her novels, including *Elinor and Marianne*, later published as *Sense and Sensibility*, *First Impressions*, renamed *Pride and Prejudice*, and *Northanger Abbey*. Other books written at Steventon in her early teens include *Love and Friendship*, *A History of England*, *A Collection of Letters* and *Lesley Castle*. We know that she would have visited The Vyne at Sherborne St John when her father worked as a locum rector there.

Jane left Steventon in 1801 to live in Bath and after her father's death in 1806 she moved to Southampton. In 1809 she returned to North Hampshire to live at Chawton and for a few weeks before her death from Addison's disease she lodged in Winchester. She died in 1817 and lies buried in Winchester Cathedral. Novels written at Chawton include *Mansfield Park*, *Emma* and *Persuasion*. It was a matter of much regret that, when the Assembly Rooms area was required for development, no attempt was made to retain the wooden structure which was consigned to the flames.

HACKWOOD PARK

ACRES OF beautiful fields and woods surround a fine house built in the closing years of the reign of James II. This is Hackwood Park, which still stands, although it is only an empty shell since the death of the last owner, Lord Camrose, in the 1990s. Until his retirement, Lord Camrose was the owner of the *Daily Telegraph*.

The original name for Hackwood was 'Hagewode', dating back to the days after the death of King John when, during the reign of Henry III, Henry de Brayboef had licence to enclose 'Hagewode' with its timber within the forest of Pamber and Eversley. This extensive forest to the north of Basingstoke was part of Windsor Great Park, through which King John often used to ride on his way to Kingsclere. Very close to Hackwood Park, on its northern side, is the spot where Danes and Saxons were once locked in battle close to the road leading to Tunworth. Skirting the northern perimeter alongside a deer park is the

Tree planting at Hackwood Park after a storm.

The 'cathedral' area of Hackwood Park being replanted in 1989 after the great storm of October 1987.

Harrow Way, part of the long route along which pilgrims passed on their way to worship at the tomb of Thomas Becket at Canterbury Cathedral.

It is interesting to note that Hackwood Park is linked to Basing House. In the 16th century it was in the possession of the Paulet family, which also owned Basing House. Sir William Paulet later became the 1st Marquis of Winchester and had his home at Basing House.

Hackwood Park has been closely associated with royalty and prime ministers. The first king to stay there was George I, who was entertained by Charles, 3rd Duke of Bolton. Baigent and Millard's *History of Basingstoke* records that the bells of St Michael's Church were rung on 28 August 1722 when the king was staying at Hackwood. The bell-ringers were paid in beer costing 2s, and in addition received 6s. The Boltons were associated with Hackwood for many years, the reason for their title being that Charles, 6th Marquis of Winchester, had been created 1st Duke of Bolton on 9 April 1689. To commemorate his visit to Hackwood George I gifted a statue of himself, which can still be seen in the park.

In July 1713, Charles, 3rd Duke of Bolton, married Lady Anne Vaughan, daughter of the Earl of Carberry. They separated a few weeks after the marriage and very soon the 3rd Duke of Bolton formed an attachment to Lavinia Fenton, one of the most famous actresses of the period, who played the part of Polly Peachum in the original production of John Gay's *The Beggar's Opera*.

Hackwood Road buildings in 1950.

The 3rd duke could not marry Lavinia until his wife died, and he had a long wait. She finally passed away on 20 September 1751, and within a month Lavinia had become the duke's second wife. As his mistress she bore him three sons, but those years since she had been little more than a teenager were very eventful ones at Hackwood. To please her the duke created the beautiful Spring Wood, with its lovely trees and delightful flowers and shrubs. Dotted around are statues and samples of Grecian architecture, which have been admired by crowds of visitors on open days. It is hoped that the new owners of Hackwood will preserve this area of outstanding beauty.

The duke and duchess had only a short time together in their married state, as the duke died on 26 August 1754. In the ensuing years, through various marriages, the dukedom of Bolton became extinct, but within a few years a gentleman by the name of Thomas Orde had married the lady who had inherited the estate. He was elevated to the peerage by George III in 1797 and revived the old name, becoming Baron Bolton of Bolton Castle. The title remains in use today.

In around 1850 the Bolton family ceased to make their home at

Hackwood Road showing thatched cottages.

Hackwood, preferring to live at Bolton Hall in Yorkshire. In 1855, the house was let to Mr Richard Bethell KC, Attorney-General and later, as Lord Westbury, to be made Lord Chancellor. The next leaseholder was Mr Charles Hoare, a banker, but when Bolton Hall was damaged by fire in around 1900, the Bolton family again took up residence at Hackwood. A later tenant was the Earl of Wilton, but the most famous tenant was Marquis Curzon of Kedleston, Viceroy of India from 1899 to 1905 and Foreign Secretary from 1919 to 1924. Lord Curzon died on 20 March 1925, after which Lady Curzon continued the tenancy until 1935. It was in this year that the 1st Lord Camrose bought the estate from the Bolton family.

During World War One, when the Germans overran Belgium, Elizabeth, queen of the Belgians, and her family were given accommodation at Hackwood Park in what was known as the Belgian Suite, in the East Wing. King Albert of Belgium visited Hackwood in 1920 and planted a tree on the east side of the lawn to commemorate his family's stay.

In 1921 the house had another famous visitor when Sir Winston Churchill, as First Lord of the Admiralty, stayed at the house to paint some of the beautiful trees and glades, among them Spring Wood.

In 1938 another famous politician stayed at Hackwood House, namely Mr Neville Chamberlain after he had returned from visiting Hitler, clutching a small piece of paper declaring 'Peace for all time'. There is a tree planted by the cricket ground commemorating the prime minister's stay.

Audley's Wood on the Alton Road, formerly an old people's home and now a hotel, is adjacent to the Hackwood estate. The house was built by Mr Bradshaw, the famous publisher of railway timetables.

During the dark days of 1940, the 1st Lord Camrose handed over a large part of the grounds and the house to the Royal Canadian Army Medical Corps for the duration of the war. The building became known as the Basingstoke Neurological and Plastic Surgery Hospital, where nearly 20,000 military patients of all nationalities were treated.

The 2nd Lord Camrose married Princess Aly Khan late in life. They both died during the 1990s and the estate and contents of the house were sold. The house, an empty shell, was bought by a wealthy Arab sheikh.

LONDON STREET CHURCH AND LONDON STREET

O NE OF Basingstoke's outstanding buildings, with its attractive façade complete with pillars of Grecian style, is in London Street, where thousands of motorists must have become very familiar with it as they drove along the A30 before the days of the Basingstoke by-pass and before the street was pedestrianised. The building is now the United Reformed Church, and was previously the Congregational Church.

Originally the Independent Church in Cross Street, it was moved to

United Reformed Church, London Street, in the days when it was the Congregational Church.

London Street in the 1920s.

London Street in 1801. The pillared front was added in 1865. The actual date that the Independent Church was founded is unknown, as the earliest records go back only as far as 1868, but it is probable that John Hooke, who lies buried in the Liten, was the minister there before 1663.

His father, William Hooke, the son of a Hampshire gentleman, was born in around 1600, entered Trinity College, Oxford on 19 May 1620 and received the degree of MA in 1623. He was instituted to the living of Upper Clatford, near Andover, on 4 May 1627. On 26 July 1632, he became vicar of Axmouth, Devon. In 1630, he married Jane Whalley, a sister of Edward Whalley, one of Cromwell's major-generals and also one of the Regicide Judges. Her mother was Frances Cromwell, an aunt of the Lord Protector.

In 1639, William Hooke became the first minister of religion in Taunton, Massachusetts. In around 1644 he moved to New Haven, Connecticut, where he remained until 1656, when he returned to his native country and became chaplain to Oliver Cromwell. On 12

January 1656 he was appointed, with Mr Caryll and Mr Sterry, to assist in a thanksgiving service for Cromwell's preservation. It was at around this time that he succeeded John Prowse as vicar of Rousdon St Pancras, Devon, near the village of Axmouth where he had previously been vicar. He appears to have been ejected from this living with the passing of the Act of Uniformity, and his successor was instituted on 8 June 1665. He died in London on 21 March 1677, leaving three sons, John, Walter and

London Street before pedestrianisation, 1952.

1930 air view showing London Street.

London Street looking from the Market Square, 1910.

Ebenezer. John Hooke had been born in 1634, attended Harvard University and left without a degree in 1652.

John probably came to England in around 1652 to benefit from the rise of Oliver Cromwell, his mother's cousin. On 3 November 1653, his father wrote from New Haven to Cromwell, thanking him for his bounty and for the favour his son had found in his eyes. It is thought that John Hooke had preached at Kingsworthy Church but there is no record in the diocesan registers. It seems likely that he was ejected from some preferment in 1662, owing to his non-acceptance of the Act of Uniformity. It is known that he then became the minister of an independent congregation in Basingstoke. On 30 July 1663, at the age of 29 years, he was chosen and admitted as one of the four chaplains of the Savoy, of which his father had been master, and held this office until the Visitation of the Savoy on 28 July 1702. Three other chaplains, John Lamb, Dean of Ely, Nicholas Onely and Lionel Coles appeared before the commission. All were discharged.

John Hooke was discharged because he was living at Basingstoke, where he was the teacher of a separate congregation from the Church of England. Dr Killegrew, then master of the Savoy, admitted that he knew John Hooke to be a dissenting preacher. Hooke died, aged 76, in

1710 and was buried in the Liten where his memorial was given the words 'This slab covers a truly reverend man, John Hooke, long time devoted to the Gospel of our Salvation, hoping for the quickening presence of the God-man; well-skilled in the Holy Scriptures, distinguished for learning, and adorned with remarkable piety'.

It is to such an outstanding man with close connections with Oliver Cromwell that the United Reformed Church in London Street owes its

London Street as it was in the late 1920s.

London Street during the reign of Edward VII.

London Road, Basingstoke, in the 1920s.

beginning. The first regular meeting of the Independents, when they assembled in 1695, adjoined the Aldworth Blue-coat School in Cross Street. Part of the building was eventually used by Mr Henry Jackson, a well known Congrgationalist, for his drapery business, and the buildings occupied by the Aldworth School subsequently became a printing works.

The new meeting place of the Independent Congregation was opened in London Street on 25 August 1801, eventually becoming the London Street Congregational Church. Toward the end of the last century, the Congregational Church in many places merged with the Presbyterian Church to become the United Reformed Church. London Street Church cost approximately £2,000 to build in 1800, and it was enlarged in 1834 and again in 1860 to provide seating for 600 people.

Toward the end of the Victorian era, the congregation included most of the influential businessmen in the town. With a remarkable administration, the church had a Sunday School over 800 strong.

London Street Church is famous for its minister in the Victorian era, John Curwen, who devised the tonic-solfa system of notation. Having great difficulty in teaching the young people attending the church the art of music, especially singing, he invented the simple tonic-solfa, which was subsequently used in schools for many years.

THE BASINGSTOKE CANAL

WHEN THE Basingstoke Canal was built in 1794, there were great hopes that the new venture would become an important part of a national network of canals which would bring to Great Britain a much cheaper way of moving cargoes. This was, of course, before the days of the railways and internal combustion engine. As it was, the last two methods of transport led to the demise of the Basingstoke Canal. However, all is not lost, for the canal from Greywell to its junction with the Wey Navigation is now a valuable leisure attraction.

A strange anomaly of the Basingstoke Canal is that it did not start from Basingstoke, but from Eastrop, a tiny parish to the east of the Hampshire town. Nevertheless, the entrance to the mooring area and to the canal basin was from Wote Street, Basingstoke, where, surprisingly, at the junction of Wote Street and Brook Street, was a weighbridge, no doubt used in connection with the barges. It is interesting that a number of barges were actually built alongside the basin of the canal, one of the most famous being named *Basingstoke*. It was *Basingstoke* that made the final trip along the canal in 1914.

To plan and open a canal was a serious business toward the end of the 18th century and required an Act of Parliament. It was as early as 1673 that the Wey Navigation was opened as far as Guildford, being extended to Godalming in 1763. It was a connection with the Wey Navigation that those planning the Basingstoke Canal were seeking.

In 1770 the first scheme to link Basingstoke with the Thames was launched. This happened two days after a public meeting was held at Reading at which it was agreed to build the Reading to Maidenhead Canal. The parliamentary committee heard the evidence in February 1771 and refused the application for the Reading-Maidenhead Canal Bill. However, it ordered that the content of the report relating to a

Basingstoke to Monkey Island Canal should be re-committed to the committee.

It was not until 1776 that Basingstoke revised its plan for a canal, and this time a link with the Thames via the Wey Navigation was proposed. In December a public meeting was held at the White Lyon, Hartford Bridge, to obtain the support of landed gentry for the project. A survey of the proposed route was made with the first estimate putting the cost at £91,118. The canal was planned to run from Cooper's Meadow in Basingstoke via Eastrop, Basing, Mapledurwell, Andwell, Nately Scures, Newnham, Rotherwick, Hartley Wespall, Turgis, Dogmersfield, Crondall, Yateley, Aldershot, Ash, Worplesdon, Pirbright, Woking and Horsell. The Wey Navigation would be joined at West Byfleet to complete a distance of 44 miles. Surprisingly, it took only three weeks for the parliamentary committee to agree that the plans complied with standing orders. Three petitions were lodged against the plans including a forceful one from the owners of Tylney Hall, Rotherwick. Nevertheless, the Bill received the Royal Assent on 15 May 1778.

The suggestion that a branch of the canal should go through Rotherwick, Turgis, Hartley Wespall and Heckfield was, however, eventually abandoned. The cutting of the main canal was begun in October 1788 from the Wey Navigation at Woodham. The canal opened at Basingstoke Wharf on 4 September 1794. It was a gigantic task costing £153,462, which was £60,000 more than the original estimate. It consisted of building 68 bridges and 29 locks, five lock houses, four wharves, three warehouses and two tunnels, with Greywell tunnel the biggest enterprise. Part of the southern wall of the tunnel collapsed in October 1874, which disrupted navigation for many months. Hundreds of navvies were employed in the construction of the canal and due to the lapse of the official copper coinage between 1775 and 1797, the Basingstoke Canal Co. issued tokens which were accepted at local shops and taverns.

Regular meetings of The Basingstoke Canal Navigation were held, some in London and others at the Crown Inn, Winchester Street, Basingstoke. During 1795, the first year of uninterrupted navigation, some 13,500 tons of freight was carried. This was at the time when the company had five barges plying the waters between Basingstoke and London. After financial problems which had threatened the viability of the canal, some stabilisation was achieved, and the company anticipated a surplus of £1,400 in the year 1807. During the first 10 years, freight carried averaged 15,000 tons per year. During the early years, when it was realised that there were few places of any size between Basingstoke and London, with Aldershot in those days having a population of only 500, there were other possible schemes to pursue, such as a connection with the Andover-Southampton Canal, or reaching the English Channel by a new route. At a meeting at the New Inn, Overton, a project was outlined for the cutting of a navigable canal from Basingstoke, via Overton and Whitchurch, to join the Andover Canal at Kitcomb Bridge. Other ideas considered were for extensions to be made out to Alton and Farnham.

In 1810, the Kennet and Avon Canal was opened, linking London and Bristol via Newbury and Bath. This gave rise for hope for a connection between Basingstoke and Newbury, with John Rennie surveying a line from Enborne near Newbury to Old Basing, via Brimpton and Kingsclere Common. If this had taken place, a possible tunnel 1,500 yards long would have been made through Tadley. This scheme obviously met with some opposition. There was also active consideration of the construction of a new ship canal for vessels of up to 400 tons from Deptford to Bristol, by way of Sydenham, Epsom and Odiham, to reach the Basingstoke Canal and eventually Devizes.

My grandfather's uncle, Samuel Attwood, wrote a diary which tells how the use of the Basingstoke Canal increased during the 19th century. His records detail the many leisure trips that he made on the canal. The diary is held at the Hampshire Record Office.

But the writing was on the wall. A new era was to break with the coming of the railways and, just as today motor traffic is competing with the railways to carry passengers and freight, so then did the railways become more than a match for the canals. However, there was a brief respite for the Basingstoke Canal, which during the building of the railway from London to Basingstoke was used to transport much material for the building of the new railway line. The cargo was carried by barges, which transported nearly 40,000 tons in 1838, an all-time peak. Sleepers, railway lines and coal comprised much of the freight. The railway line ran close to the canal.

With the line completed to Basingstoke by June 1839, and to Southampton by 11 May 1840, traffic on the waterway began to decline severely. A further unexpected stay of execution occurred when it was

Basingstoke Canal.

found that the new Aldershot Camp was to be built alongside the Basingstoke Canal, which meant that the tons of material needed for the many buildings were mainly transported by barges.

In later years, another attempt to create freight traffic was made by building a kiln at Up Nateley and excavating an arm of the canal where as many as nine barges could be moored. This is now referred to as the Brickmakers Arm. Close by, what remains of a longboat which was used on the canal in the 1860s lies beneath the shallow waters and at times, during a dry season, lies partly exposed.

The Greywell tunnel had been very problematic, with a serious collapse occurring in late Victorian days. In 1932, another major collapse occurred, which greatly reduced the likelihood of freight traffic being renewed to Basingstoke. Today it is still impossible to navigate the complete length of the tunnel.

Between 1869 and 1910, the speculators busied themselves and several sales were arranged for the Basingstoke Canal and its considerable, associated properties. Commercial traffic to and from Basingstoke ended in 1901. There was an attempt in 1913 to determine how navigable the canal still was. The barge employed for this purpose was the aptly named *Basingstoke,* and loaded with nothing but five tons of sand, she left Ash Vale on 16 November. Progress was hard through the reeds, but on reaching Slade's bridge at Up Nateley the lack of water forced the barge to heave to. The attempt had to be completely abandoned at the King's Head. A differing report of its progress appeared in the *Hants & Berks Gazette,* which said that the barge did reach Basingstoke eventually but only after water was poured into the shallow spots.

The canal's potential for pleasure boating was soon realised and today it is widely used as far as the east end of Greywell Tunnel. A considerable amount of the restoration work has been done by volunteer canal enthusiasts. Hampshire County Council purchased a stretch of the canal from the Greywell Tunnel to Penny Bridge in 1990, with Surrey County Council being responsible for the establishment of a Canal Centre at Mytchett. *John Pinkerton*, named after the builder of the canal, is the name of the pleasure boat employed in regular excursions.

Before the close of the 20th century, impressed by the support and voluntary help of the Surrey and Hampshire Canal Society, Basingstoke and Deane Council carried out a feasibility study to give the canal a focal point in Basingstoke, following proposals by the former mayor of Basingstoke, Keith Chapman. This would enable boating to take place as far as Old Basing.

Watson's buses.

COACHES

IN THE 18th century, horse-drawn transport formed a vital part of the very primitive transport and communications infrastructure of the period. There was no competition from railways or the motor car and of course, in those days, the telephone had yet to be invented. What was so remarkable was the fact that this mode of transportation ran to a timetable, 24 hours a day. Horse-drawn wagons conveyed freight only and the stage coaches conveyed passengers with some taking mail as well. The operators depended on the services supplied by publicans, hoteliers and ostlers, who looked after the horses and supplied replacements at various stages en route.

The mail coaches ran a regular service under the heading of post days. The mail coach would arrive from London on Sunday, Wednesday and Friday at approximately 6pm, with the London-bound coach setting off from Basingstoke between 8 and 9pm on Sunday, Tuesday and Thursday.

The inns used for the stage coaches included the Wheatsheaf at Winton Square, the Three Tuns on the corner of Winchester Street and Victoria Street, the Red Lion, London Street, the George in the Market Place commonly known as 'The Hole in the Wall', the Feathers, Wote Street, the Crown, Winchester Street, the Angel, Market Place and the Blue Anchor in London Street.

The Salisbury coach stopped at the Three Tuns en route to London every night at about 10pm, and the return coach called at the Red Lion every morning at 2am. There was also a Salisbury light coach running every day from the Wheatsheaf at 10pm and returning at one in the morning. There were four Exeter coaches for the hoteliers and ostlers to tend to. The post coach stopped at the George every night at 11pm, with one returning at 3am. The Exeter diligence coach stopped at the Wheatsheaf every morning at 7am on its way to London, and the return coach arrived back at 8pm.

There was a stage coach from Southampton passing through every

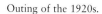

Outing of the 1920s.

day except Sunday at approximately 10am, with the return coach arriving at approximately 12 noon. There was also a Bath and Bristol coach breakfasting every morning on its way to London at the Crown, with the return coach booked in to dine at 3pm.

In addition to passenger traffic there were various wagons running between London and Exeter, Taunton and Salisbury on various days every week. Times of arrival were also varied, meaning that the catering staff and those looking after the horses literally had to work round the clock.

In some cases it was possible not to see a stage coach in during normal business hours.

Of the inns named, the Crown and the Angel closed many years ago and, like the Three Tuns, which closed in Edwardian times, the buildings still survive. The Feathers, the Red Lion and the George are still in business today, but the Blue Anchor is no more and the building has been demolished. The stage coaches became redundant soon after the arrival of the railway in early Victorian times.

RIOTS, ELECTIONS AND STRIKES

BASINGSTOKE has not been free from riots as visitors to The Vyne, the National Trust mansion, will know, for in the ante-chapel can be seen, neatly stored away, 68 truncheons. They date from 1830, when people were rising up against the Corn Laws, and there were riots in Basingstoke town centre, At the time, Mr Wiggett Chute lived at The Vyne and in his position as lord of the manor, he thought that he must do something to help keep the peace should there be any aggressive protests at Sherborne St John. In that village there was a section of the militia, the East Sherborne section, who could fall back on the truncheons in the event of trouble.

There was an earlier riot during the Napoleonic campaign in 1797 when news was received, by means of beacons being lit, that Nelson had defeated the French Fleet at Cape St Vincent. Normally when good news was received the local populace would celebrate. A popular method was to decorate houses and shops, or 'to paint the town red' and this is what the younger element did with great enthusiasm. However, not all of the townspeople were keen to celebrate in this way, including Mr Wallis.

Mr Wallis was a Quaker and he refused to join in the celebrations and decorate his house in the Market Square. The crowds gathered in the Market Square did not care much for his attitude but chose, on this occasion, to refrain from taking any action.

People, like elephants, have long memories and this was proved in October 1805, when the beacons at Farleigh Hill and Beacon Hill were again lit to celebrate the great victory over the French at Trafalgar which cost Horatio Nelson his life. The crowds of Basingstoke's younger citizens made a beeline for Mr Wallis's house and threatened him if he did not join in the celebrations. Mr Wallis, however, a man true to his word, stood his ground and refused to celebrate in any way. Without further ado, the crowd made use of the cobblestones in the Market Square and proceeded to smash every window on Mr Wallis's property.

The police force, which numbered only five constables, dared not intervene, and the superintendent of police had no option but to ask for the Riot Act to be read. This posed problems, for the mayor had to read the Riot Act and he was out of town visiting Eastrop, a separate parish on the eastern perimeter of Basingstoke.

He was located and brought back to the Market Place where, to reinforce the action he was taking, he ordered the Carabiniers to turn out and clear the streets. This territorial unit, which had only been formed in 1793, smartly obliged.

There was a sequel. In those days, the parish council was responsible for keeping law and order and for paying for any damage. Mr Wallis sent them a bill for £6 16s 9d to pay for the cost of reglazing the windows of his property. This is duly recorded in the parish accounts for that year which can be seen at the Hampshire Record Office at Winchester. In those days, the church was responsible for administering the Poor Law, road maintenance, the appointing of night-watchmen and the administration of the Fire Brigade. The fire engine was kept at St Michael's Church.

These uprisings were nothing compared to what happened during the Salvation Army Riots which occurred between December 1880 and March 1882. When the Salvation Army first came to the town, they

The home of Mr J.B. Soper after being stoned by the rioters during the Salvation Army riots.

used the old Silk Mill building in Brook Street, which was later demolished as part of town development in the 1960s.

The problem was that Basingstoke had a bad reputation for drunkenness, which had been brought to the notice of General Booth, head of the Salvation Army. At the time, Basingstoke had a population of 6,681, served by over 50 public houses. To preach the folly of strong drink, General Booth sent 25 Salvation Army lassies with some officers who worked from what was termed their 'workshop' in the old Silk Mill.

The Salvation Army crackdown on strong drink was strongly resisted by the three brewers in the town, with the most influential being John May's brewery in Brook Street. The brewery stood on the site now occupied by the Anvil, Basingstoke's modern concert hall. The brewers feared a drop in their profits and their employees were anxious lest they lost their employment as a result.

The Salvation Army had the backing of a number of leading town folk and the churches, especially the London Street Congregational Church. Opposing the Salvation Army was an organisation known as the Massaganians, supported and egged on by the brewers. The *Basingstoke Gazette* also supported the Salvation Army, especially Mr John Bird, proprietor and editor of the paper.

After the Massaganians had been denounced in the columns of the *Gazette*, a large stone was thrown through the window of the newspaper's office. The man responsible was rewarded by the brewers with a gallon of ale. Mrs Bird, wife of the founder of the paper, was cut by a glass splinter.

After the Salvation Army arrived in Basingstoke, they paraded through the town, holding open-air meetings and services, spreading their message of abstinence from alcohol. Much ill-feeling simmered and many incidents occurred during December 1880. Whenever mob violence broke out with some of those taking part being under the influence of alcohol, many people were shocked. Cases of people being clubbed on the head, hurled on to railings or 'ducked' in the Basingstoke Canal alarmed the population. Captain Jordan of the Salvation Army had a narrow escape when, on his way to the railway station, he was waylaid by a party of ruffians led by a Mr Fitzgerald. He was about to be thrown into the River Loddon at the bottom of Wote Street when, by good fortune, the police arrived. The shallow stream was some five feet below the pavement and had the captain been dumped there, he would probably have died.

Diarist George W. Woodman recorded what actually happened in his diary, now held by the Willis Museum. He wrote:

> On the morning of Sunday, March 20, 1881, between nine and ten, some 200 or so of the roughest characters in the town collected in the Market Place for the purpose of molesting the Salvation Army. Most of them had sticks under their arms and short pipes in their mouths. The numbers greatly increased until it reached about 1,000. At the same time, many more respectable people went out and headed the Salvation Army and protected them on either side. What happened was disgraceful. Some of the Salvation Army supporters tried to keep their footings, others tried to push them down. Some windows were smashed in Church Street. In the afternoon, about 1.40pm, the mob, a drunken rabble, assembled again. They forced the Salvation Army into Church Square and broke their ranks. They knocked their heads about with sticks, kicked them and many of them, being drunk, would have made short work of the Salvationists but for the timely aid of sympathisers.
>
> …I saw a man led away with his arm broken and head cut, another man with his neck bleeding and another with his head cut open. There were bleeding heads and faces in all directions. On this occasion, the police and Mayor, W.H. Blatch, himself a brewer, stood by and did nothing. Among the leaders of the mob were the Adams brothers from the Victoria Brewery.
>
> …John Burgess Soper, Arkas Soper, the Rev Barron of the London Street Congregational Church, Richard Wallis and other members of the Wallis family were attacked as they walked with the Salvation Army.

Superintendent Hibberd, head of the Basingstoke police, realised what was going to happen with only five policemen in his force and so he applied to the mayor for a body of special constables. As a result 100 men were recruited, coming from all walks of life. On Sunday 27 March at 9.30am, the special constables assembled at the Town Hall to receive their badges of office and their batons. Soon after 10am, the Salvation

Army came marching up with police special constables in front, at the rear and on either side.

Mr Woodman wrote:

> in the afternoon, I went to the Silk Mill in Brook Street and saw the Salvation Army outside, four deep, and ready to move off, but the Mayor stopped them as he was afraid of the mob – there were at least 3,000 people in Brook Street and Church Street.

The scene before lunch had been very grave. As the Salvation Army marched back to the Silk Mill, they were followed by the Massaganians, who were blowing trumpets, rattling pot lids and singing obscene songs. They all went down Wote Street and all seemed to be passing off well, but some of the special constables returned to the Town Hall and swore that they would not protect such a set of 'damned hypocrites'.

The climax came as Mr Woodman described:

> The Riot Act was read from the Town Hall and the Royal Horse Artillery, who were spending the weekend in Basingstoke, had orders to clear the streets, some on horseback and some on foot with the special constables. The soldiers on horseback took up the whole width of the road and pavement, allowing nobody to stand on their own doorstep. They cleared everything before them.

The rioting was so severe that it formed the subject of a question in the House of Commons.

On Tuesday 12 April 1881, the Old Angel Café was opened in the Market Place. It was on the site of the Angel Inn, one of the old coaching houses, which had closed in 1866 and then been used as a draper's shop and warehouse.

The new café was a temperance café, and just after the vicar had declared it open and was drinking a cup of tea, one of the Massaganians put his head inside and bawled out something, 'nobody knew what', to quote Mr Woodman.

On 30 August, Mr Woodman wrote in his diary:

> in the morning at 10am, 20 persons were summonsed to appear before the magistrates for assault and obstruction. A number of Massaganians had assembled, they became most uproarious, shouting, hissing, yelling, beating drums, cymbals and waving rattles. When the magistrates court had

finished, they surrounded one of the magistrates, obstructed the way, blew a horn in his face, and would have killed him if they had dared. Ten rioters were sent to jail.

On 21 September 1881, Mr Woodman wrote:

Return of the Massaganians from Winchester Jail. They were fetched home in carriages with postillions. They had a band of hundreds of people to welcome them home, with flags flying and strings of flags across Winchester Street. Dinner was held for them in the Corn Exchange and each received a silver watch. The Corn Exchange (now the Haymarket Theatre) was crammed full and the noise they kicked up was awful.

An election was held on 1 November 1881. Mr Woodman recorded the event thus:

Municipal Election – A fiercely contested one, the first time it had been fought out politically. Torys against Liberals, Churchmen against dissenters, temperance against drink, Massaganians against the Salvation Army. The Massaganians gained the day. A mob of about 200 went up to London

General Booth visits Basingstoke. He is seen here near Winton Square.

Salvation Army riots, 1882. Damage to window of the *Gazette* office.

Street to annoy, then went down Church Street and smashed windows at the *Gazette* office and other windows, then made a mad rush down to the Congregational Minister's house and smashed his windows. Then on to the old Silk Mill where 200 Salvationists were holding a meeting with Major Moore. The mob attacked the building, tried to break through the

A declaration of poll at the Town Hall.

The Basingstoke Strike Committee, formed during the 1926 General Strike.

door, smashed all the windows and attacked the roof. The mob then went up Chapel Street to South View and tried to break into Mr Soper's house and to set fire to the place, but were unsuccessful. The mob smashed every window.

A few months later, Mr Woodman wrote:

Sunday, March 5, 1882, Rioting again – a most disgraceful scene. The Superintendent assured the magistrates that, with his five men, he was able to quell any riot that may occur.

What were five or six policemen against a mob of 2,000, asked Mr Woodman, whose later entries showed that, from that date onwards, the ill-feeling and disturbances gradually died down.

THE RAILWAYS

F OR THE past 150 years Basingstoke has been a railway town. At one time the railways employed many men, so many that railway cottages were built to house railway families. A terrace still stands in Lower Brook Street.

It was in June 1839 that the railway reached the Hampshire town. Hundreds of navvies were employed to cut through the chalk. Part of the line in the Basingstoke area was laid through the highest plateau on the London and Southampton Railway.

When the line was constructed from London, Shapley Heath near Winchfield became a temporary terminus for passenger trains. The railway spelt the end for the stage coaches which ran to strict timetables between London, Salisbury, Bath and Taunton before reaching Exeter.

Holy Ghost ruins looking east to where Whistler's windmill stood 1826–48. In the background on the right is the original Basingstoke railway station.

The proprietors of the stage coaches, realising that they would soon be out of business, ran their coaches to connect with the trains at Shapley Heath.

It was great for travellers to sample rail transport but they were not prepared to put up with much discomfort. From their padded coaches they took their seats on the train in what were little better than cattle trucks, with no roof for protection from the weather. Furthermore, the high chimneys of those primitive locomotives belched out red-hot cinders and ashes that often dropped upon the passengers.

After the line was opened to Basingstoke, there was some opposition to rail travel and daytrips were run for a few pence to Old Basing where a temporary platform was erected. It was another year before the railway reached Southampton, the delay being caused by the high ground between Basingstoke and Winchester. In order to keep gradients at a minimum, no fewer than four tunnels were constructed between Basingstoke and Winchester and in several locations deep cuttings and high embankments were necessary.

Basingstoke was to become an important junction from where almost any part of England, Wales and Scotland could be reached by rail, but there were snags. Head of the Great Western Railway was Isambard Kingdom Brunel, a great champion of the broad gauge, which ran from Basingstoke to Reading. This meant that travellers had to change trains and gauge if they wanted to use the Reading line, which opened in 1848. This was a great hindrance to travellers, including Queen Victoria who had to change trains whenever she was en route from Windsor Castle to the Isle of Wight. It took various Acts of Parliament in order for conformity of gauge to be effected. Eventually the broad gauge was abandoned and standard gauge won the day. By 1869, the broad gauge from Basingstoke to Reading had been abandoned, making it easier for Basingstoke travellers to reach Wales, the Midlands, the North and Scotland.

A great advance for local travellers came in July 1860, when the route to Andover, Salisbury and Exeter was fully opened. This route opened in stages. The section from Basingstoke to Salisbury was opened in 1857 and that from Salisbury to Gillingham in 1859, and then on to Exeter. All

The first train on the Basingstoke and Alton Light Railway.

The Battledown flyover is negotiated by trains on the Bournemouth and Exeter route.

The first train on the Basingstoke and Alton Railway.

Basingstoke railway station, 1902.

Station Hill as many remember it, before redevelopment.

these connections from Basingstoke were also vital for goods traffic, especially for the conveyance of coal.

Eventually, Basingstoke had two stations – one for London and the West from the main London and South Western station and one for the Great Western Railway serving Reading and the other GWR stations. The main Basingstoke station had a large goods station and engine station. Over the years, many fine locomotives could be seen at the Basingstoke shed and for boys, a great attraction was to see mighty

Basing Viaduct near the old mill restaurant.

Pacific locos being turned on the turntable. The light parcel office by the main platform was a very busy place, with thousands of parcels handled daily.

Today, the engine shed, goods shed, marshalling yard and parcel deliveries are a thing of the past and the station handles hundreds of

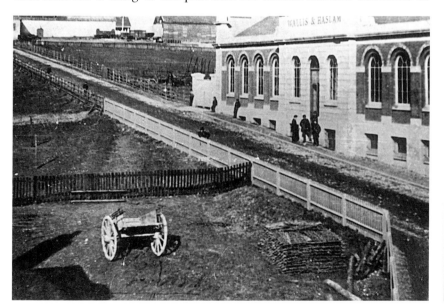

Station Hill as it was in the 1860s, showing Wallis and Haslam's engineering works, whose static steam engines, traction engines and road rollers were built.

Basingstoke railway station following development after the removal of the cattle market.

commuters every week-day instead. The station has been modernised on at least three occasions.

The last century saw two branch lines opened, the Basingstoke and Alton Light Railway in 1901 and a single track to Park Prewett Psychiatric Hospital in 1913. The Alton line closed in 1935 and the Park Prewett line in the 1950s. At one time, the rural stations outside Basingstoke had goods sheds and sidings where shunting was done by locos from Basingstoke.

Today, with many people living in the villages and many of them commuters, the talk is of stations being opened at Chineham and Oakley, the latter having been a victim of the Beeching pruning.

THE LIGHT RAILWAY

NO RECORD of Basingstoke's history would be complete without reference to the Basingstoke and Alton Light Railway, probably the most famous light railway in Great Britain. It was on the Basingstoke and Alton Light Railway that two films, *The Wrecker* and *Oh! Mr Porter*, the latter starring Will Hay, Moore Marriott and Graham Moffatt, were partly made.

Apart from the filming, the line itself makes for quite a historical contribution, which is still remembered by Basingstoke's elderly citizens. At the end of the 19th century there was much talk about the construction of a line from the Great Western Railway at Basingstoke and another from Guildford which would meet at Alton. This would have cost £2,000,000 and was opposed by the London and South Western Railway and also by the London, Brighton and South Coast Railway.

The London and South Western Railway had other ideas and in 1897 sought powers under the Light Railways Act of 1896, to build a line from Basingstoke to connect with the Mid-Hants line at the Butts Bridge, Alton.

The 12.5-mile length of track required was not an easy project, especially at the Basingstoke end. A deep cutting was necessary near Worting Road. The chalk excavated from this cutting was used to construct a long embankment which was required to take the line from Basingstoke Station to the side of Thornycroft's motor works. The new line was in place as far as Herriard and from Lasham to Alton by March 1900 but, because of problems, the line was not complete from Basingstoke Station to Butts Junction, Alton until the summer of 1901. The line was officially opened on Saturday 21 June. There were three intermediate stations, namely Cliddesden, Herriard and Lasham and Bentworth.

The number of passengers conveyed was disappointing, according to the *Basingstoke Gazette,* but the paper reminded its readers that traffic was disappointing in 1840 when the first trains ran to Southampton 'but the number of passengers using the main line today is a good sign and who knows what will be the support in 40 years time?'

We have known the answer for many years. During World War One the track was lifted for use in France and to get the line re-opened a Bill in Parliament was necessary. In 1923, a Bill was brought before Parliament seeking powers to abandon the line. This was opposed by principal landowners, farmers and public bodies who organised a petition to have the track reinstated and the route re-opened. The petition was successful and the re-opening took place on 18 August 1924. The first train on that day was driven by Mr W. Hudson, assisted by Mr A. Willett, fireman and Mr H. Tiller, guard, all from the Basingstoke depot.

After the re-opening, when there were only three trains a day serving Alton and the intermediate stations, criticism began to grow about the limited service. The line proved to be far from viable and closed to passenger traffic at the end of the summer season in 1932. Freight traffic lingered on until 1 June 1936 when the line was finally closed to all traffic.

However, the line was far from finished. A few years previously on Sunday 19 August 1928, one of the most violent rail crashes ever staged for a film took place at the railway crossing at Lasham Hill Farm. It was for a film aptly entitled *The Wrecker*. A newspaper report described the crash: '...travelling at 50 miles an hour an express train dashed into a steam lorry at a level crossing near Basingstoke in order to supply a realistic touch for the film version of *The Wrecker* for Gainsborough Pictures Ltd.'

The Southern Railway had sold to the producer a six-coach bogie set train and an ex-South Eastern Railway tender locomotive. The report in the *Basingstoke Gazette* said:

> United Coast Lines had been painted on the tender. After rehearsing for several hours up and down the track with the train and the Foden steam wagon, everything was in place for the final masterpiece. The foden wagon was placed across the track. The engine of the doomed train was in charge of Driver J. Brown and Fireman G. Goodright, both of Guildford. The Director gave the signal to the linesman, the regulator was opened with full steam ahead. The driver

Cliddesden Station, featured in the film *Oh! Mr Porter*.

shouted to his fireman to jump, before leaping from the footplate himself. In 65 seconds it was all over. The speed at the point of impact was about 45 miles an hour. There was a terrible explosion heard a mile away. Smoke and sparks shot 15 feet into the air. After ploughing up the track for 120 yards, the engine fell on its side, a perfect wreck. At 3pm the Director and cameramen were ready to rescue 'passengers' from the wrecked train. An hour later a large van loaded with cans of petrol arrived which was poured on the train and set on fire, presenting a very interesting but pitiful picture. The cost of the day's work was put at £7,000. Within 24 hours the debris had been cleared and the track relaid to enable the 3.25pm Basingstoke to Alton train to pass. The story of the crash was carried by all the daily papers.

In June 1937 another Gainsborough production was filmed on the line with Will Hay, Moore Marriott and Graham Moffatt surprising visitors to Cliddesden where the station had been renamed 'Buggleskelly'. Three locomotives were loaned for the film, an Adams class X2 4-4-0 built in 1895, an Adams 0-6-0 built in 1885 and a 2-4-0 tank engine named *Northiam* which, for the film, was renamed *Gladstone*. Mr George Stevens of Basingstoke was fireman on the Adams X2 locomotive and also took part in another film made at Basingstoke entitled the *Honeymoon Express,* starring Claude Hulbert. George Stevens was a neighbour of the author who knew him well.

Cliddesden station was completely transformed for the filming with the mouth of a tunnel created. The film stars thoroughly enjoyed themselves in such a rural setting and Graham Moffatt treated the Southern Railway staff to ice-cream.

It was a great experience for Cliddesden people and in order to create a scene of Graham Moffatt milking a cow, local farmer Ernest Hooper rigged up a contrivance. He also loaned one of his cows, which nearly caused a panic when it jumped through a carriage window. The film gave Cliddesden unexpected fame, with people still visiting the village to view the remaining trackbed and to catch a glimpse of the site of the station.

Until 1967, both ends of the Basingstoke and Alton line were in use. A short stub at the Basingstoke end was used as a siding serving Thornycroft's motor works, while a similar short stub at the Butts Junction end was used to convey coal to the adjacent Lord Mayor Treloar's Hospital.

Parts of the old track-bed can still be seen, running through picturesque countryside between Cliddesden, Bentworth, Lasham and the approach to Alton.

The rather dilapidated Bentworth and Lasham station building can be clearly seen from the A339 Basingstoke to Alton road.

BASINGSTOKE MYSTERIES

LIKE MOST towns, Basingstoke has had its fair share of reports of ghosts and strange happenings. A poltergeist is said to have performed all manner of antics in a house at Warton Road, on the Southview estate. Both the occupants and the next door neighbours reported witnessing the events. Stones on the floor seemed to appear from nowhere and objects in the kitchen were moved. The occupants, although very frightened, continued to live in their home.

The Haymarket Theatre reportedly houses a ghost that can sometimes be seen walking in the darkened auditorium in daytime.

One incident for which I have no explanation was reported in an issue of the *Hants & Berks Gazette* in Victorian times.

At the time there were small chapels in the outlying villages which relied on visiting lay preachers from Basingstoke to conduct their services. There were many local preachers who worked to a local preachers' plan. A lay preacher was returning to Basingstoke on foot from the tiny chapel at Newfound, near Oakley. He was more than halfway on his journey, on a road where there were no houses, when suddenly he noticed a figure clad in white, walking ahead. The lay preacher wondered who it could be walking along the dark road. He tried to overtake the figure, but before he could do so, the figure jumped over a hedge at the spot where Basingstoke Fire Station is today, and disappeared.

The lay preacher, very shaken, eventually arrived at the little wooden chapel in Potters Lane and climbed the outside steps into the room used for worship where, looking very pale and haggard, still shaking from his experience, he was met by the minister. He had difficulty in relating what had happened.

A similar event a month later was experienced by another preacher and was again duly recorded in the *Hants & Berks Gazette*. I may have a sequel to the story, for West Ham Lane, which runs from Worting to Basingstoke, does appear to be haunted. I was asked about this by the manager and an employee of the ten-pin bowling alley just off West Ham Lane some three years ago – they wanted to know if there had been any murders in that vicinity. I had to tell them that there had, for a teenage girl was murdered in one of the fields nearby some 40 years ago. Also, early one morning in the 1920s, the severely mutilated body of a man was found hanging from a fence in that area. In the 1970s I had a faithful collie dog named Laddie, who would do everything he could not to go through West Ham Lane. If off the lead, he would run 200 yards past the opening to the lane in order to avoid walking through it. Since then I have had two other dogs who would go through the lane without any qualms.

On two occasions a ghost was seen outside the old Swan Inn in Wote Street. Some of the customers kept watch and saw a figure draped in white emerging from a house in New Road. The figure was then followed and eventually apprehended outside the inn, where he was not treated very gently!

Old sayings live on in Basingstoke. For many years people have told the story of how at midnight on New Year's Eve, King George I and his horse would leave the statue outside Hackwood House and gallop round the park.

When I was churchwarden I was approached by a young housewife, a stranger to me, but who lived in the same street, and asked if I could get a priest to exorcise her bedroom where, she was told, someone had been murdered. One of the team vicars obliged, the Revd Bill Ind, who is now Bishop of Truro. I am sure she had been dreaming for no murder has been committed in the street in which I have lived for 80 years.

There was once a young curate at St Michael's Church who told me that he did not like entering St Michael's after dark for 'it is spooky', he said. He would know that hundreds of people have been buried beneath the church.

One mystery that has long been associated with Basingstoke is linked to *Ruddigore*, one of the Savoy operas, by Gilbert and Sullivan. The opera contains the word 'Basingstoke', which is said to have a hidden meaning. One of the characters, 'Mad Margaret', is apt to lapse into insanity. Whenever she does so, she is asked by Sir Despard Murgatroyd to immediately say the word 'Basingstoke', to drive away the madness. When urged to say the word with a hidden meaning, she would reply, 'Basingstoke! And so it is!'

Ruddigore has been performed several times by the Thornycroft and Basingstoke Amateur Operatic Society with the players often wondering why the word 'Basingstoke' was chosen by Gilbert. The idea was that there was a mad-house in Basingstoke where Mad Margaret would have to go if she became utterly insane, so it was a frightening word. It is believed that Gilbert was staying at Farnborough when he wrote the operetta. At the time, Basingstoke had a pest house, or hospital for those with infectious diseases, which was located off the Victory Square and remained in use until the end of the Victorian era. How apt it would have been if Gilbert had written the story some 20 years later, for Basingstoke was to have the largest psychiatric hospital in Hampshire at Park Prewett. In recent years the hospital has been closed and has been replaced by 'Parklands', a modern in-patient unit close to the general hospital site.

MUMMERS

WITHOUT entertainment in the home as is available today, by the operating of a switch, our ancestors, without any acting experience, set about giving their own entertainments which became very popular around Christmas time. They were the Mummers, who were very strong in North Hampshire, especially in the Overton and Whitchurch areas. The performers were groups of village folk whose stage was normally a pub. Overton was one village famed for its Mummers and they ranged far and wide to perform their strange plays featuring St George and the Turkish Knight. They received great support in Basingstoke.

A Mr Fred Randall, of East Oakley, had an account of the Hampshire Mummers written by his father in 1912. Even by that time, performances by Mummers were becoming very scarce, for he wrote:

> Most of our old south country customs such as the observance of feasts, maypole dances, backwoodsmanship, Mummers and other quaint diversions, have more or less disappeared from Hampshire village life. But you find traces of those old time forms of recreation in a few of our out of the way villages where railways have never reached. Where the truly rural mind, cultivated by village hall lectures, or street corner orators, is content to browse and ruminate in its own pasture. Many of the old folk still reckon dates from Feast Day Monday and the maypole is, or was, of refreshing fruit fame, erected at club feasts. It is possible you may still find a few small bands of so-called Mummers, who gabble a few rhymes and smite each other with wooden swords. The merry, dare devil Mummers of 35 years ago, which I can still remember, are no more to be seen.

He continued:

> Thirty or more years ago, in my native village of Vernham Deane on the downs near the Wiltshire border, the

Mummers flourished their swords mightily and played with great spirit the act of St George and the Turkish Knight and were an indispensable part of the Christmas festivities at family gatherings and public houses. The players were village lads, from workshop or plough and were always keen on doing their very best. The fighting men carried real swords, blunted for the occasion, all were fantastically dressed in gaily ribboned costumes, more or less appropriate to the character being played. They wore dark or blue trousers with red stripes, white shirts tucked in over their underclothes and a waistcoat, for a headdress, they wore a conical white hat crowned with red and blue streamers. The Mummers were always word-perfect, they never lacked spirit and sometimes acted really well.

Describing the arrival of the Mummers, he wrote:

The Mummers have come across the green and now take their stand before an open door and begin to sing the opening carol. The first verse was

'God bless the mistress of the house.
        With gold across her breasts.
Oh, let her body be sleep or awake.
        God send her soul to rest'.

The first Mummer to enter was usually the Turkish Knight who would say, 'Room and room and gallons of room, make room for me my swing and let old Father Christmas in'. On entering, Father Christmas said, 'In comes I, old Father Christmas, Christmas or Christmas not, I hope old Father Christmas will never be forgot. For room and room I require this night, to see these two bold champions fight'.

St George, on entering said, 'In comes I, St George, the man of courage bold, with my spear I gained the crowns of gold. I fought the fiery dragon and brought him to the slaughter and by these holy means, I gained the King of Egypt's daughter. Walk in the Turkish, act thy part, show the ladies and gentlemen thy stubborn heart'.

The Turkish Knight accepts the challenge by saying, 'In comes I, the Turkish Knight, just come from the Turkish land to fight. I'll fight thee St George, the man of courage bold and if thy blood runs fast, I'll quickly draw it cold'.

In the fight that follows, the Turkish Knight is cut down by St George. Father Christmas then enters and says, 'Oh, St George, what hast thou done, thou hast ruined me by slaying my son'.

A doctor then appears on the scene, who, when asked what he can cure, replies 'I can cure the itch, the stitch, the palsy and the gout, all pains within and without. I carry a little bottle by my left side which is called the hop pop and the smoke by day and the alley-campaign by night, which will heal the sick and bring this dead man to life again'.

Three other characters arrive on the scene to complete the act, the Cutting Star, Twing Twang Press Gang and Saucy Jack, who sums it all up by saying, 'A mug of your good Christmas ale, will make us all merry and sing, A little more money in our pocket, is a very fine thing. A mug of your ale, if it's not too stale, and fill it right up to the brim, and then we will all drink and sing, a merry Christmas hymn'. This would often be *Good King Wenceslas*. To finish off the evening, there would be elder wine, strong ale, bread and cheese and songs by the company.

I was too young to be admitted to a Basingstoke pub to see the Mummers but I can remember seeing the characters outside a pub. I believe it was the New Inn at the bottom of Sarum Hill.

THE MAY FAMILY

Lt-Col John May, mayor of Basingstoke six times and a generous benefactor. This is the only known phothgraph of him.

O NE OF the most illustrious names in Basingstoke's history is that of Lt-Col John May, who is surely worthy of the title of the town's greatest benefactor. He was a wealthy man, with great foresight, to whom lovers of cricket owe a great debt.

When Queen Victoria's reign was drawing to a close, he knew that a piece of land to the south of the town, off what was called Back Lane, was required for house building. Lt-Col May had other ideas. A keen sportsman, he thought that the piece of ground, which was in a very picturesque setting, would make an ideal cricket pitch. At the time, Basingstoke had no cricket or football grounds. The latter sport was played on Basingstoke Common. As for cricket, the place to see good class cricket was Hackwood Park.

Within a remarkably short time, Lt-Col May had arranged for the All England team to play at what was called the Folly, against 24 men of North Hampshire. The Folly, later to be renamed May's Bounty in honour of the great man who had donated it, has given thousands of people great pleasure, players and spectators alike. For many years, county cricket has been played on the ground, which has been greatly admired by leading Test players and county elevens. Unfortunately, in 2000, the last county game was played there. Hampshire have now moved to a new county ground in Southampton. With good crowds turning up at May's Bounty, it is just possible that the Hampshire Cricket Club's decision may be reversed.

Not only cricketers owe a debt to Lt-Col May, who was head of the brewing company of John May & Co., founded in 1751 and eventually bought by Simonds, the Reading brewers, in 1951. Lt-Col May was elected mayor, and proved so generous in the position that he held the office on six occasions, three of them coinciding with years of celebrations – Queen Victoria's Jubilee in 1887, her Diamond Jubilee in 1897 and the Coronation of King Edward VII and Queen Alexandra in 1902.

The family of John May.

During his mayoralty in 1887, he donated to Basingstoke the huge clock which looked over the town for 80 years. Unfortunately, the structure of the Town Hall was giving grave cause for concern, and the ageing building no longer able to carry such a great weight. In 1961 the clock was dismantled.

As mayor, Lt-Col May carried on a great tradition. His ancestors had held the office of mayor of Basingstoke 15 times between 1711 and 1839. He was only 26 when he was first elected as a town councillor, and 20 years later, he was elected mayor for the first time.

The immediate ancestors, who founded the brewing business, of Lt-Col May are thought to have originated in Brimpton. It is known, however, that there were Mays living in Basingstoke 450 years ago, for the name occurs among a list of the members of the Guild of the Holy Ghost in 1557.

Records show that the May family continued living in Basingstoke and in the churchwarden's accounts for 1622 there is a record of Jasper May paying 2s for the ringing of the knell at his wife's death. Also, in around 1685, a John May of Worting married Elizabeth Coleman. It is thought that this John May was possibly a brother of the first May to become mayor of Basingstoke.

Lt-Col John May was born in Church Street on 3 June 1837, a few days before Queen Victoria came to the throne. At the time, the population of Basingstoke was only about 4,000, so it could be said that

Drillhall, Sarum Hill, built and presented to Basingstoke by Lt-Col John May.

he grew up with the town. He was educated firstly at Queen Mary's School, when the school was within the precincts of the Holy Ghost Chapel. Subsequently he attended War Field Grove, near Bracknell, then Tunbridge Wells and finally Southampton. While at Southampton, he saw troops leaving for the Crimean War, which so inspired him with military ardour that it was only his widowed mother who prevented him from enlisting. He was a great sportsman and developed a passion for hunting and kept a stable of hunters.

His most serious time of life was with the volunteer forces and for 40 years he had a very close connection with the forces. At the age of 22 he moved a resolution at the Town Hall to form the Basingstoke Corps of the Hampshire Volunteers, which he joined and was eventually gazetted ensign. In 1864 he transferred to the Hampshire Militia in which he rose to the rank of captain. In 1878 he returned to the militia, eventually rising to become an honorary major and eventually an honorary lieutenant colonel.

Houses and out-buildings forming part of John May's brewery.

Basingstoke was without a drill hall but Lt-Col May rectified this by building one at the top of Sarum Hill, which became the leading hall in Basingstoke. It was here that many balls, bazaars and exhibitions were held and it was the favourite venue for the Hunt Ball. The hall remained in use until the 1960s. For some years it was the Plaza Cinema, eventually becoming the Basingstoke Co-operative Society's furniture department.

Gradually, civic duties took up most of May's time. When Lord Roberts came home from South Africa, Lt-Col May was presented to him at the railway station. Lord Roberts expressed his great pleasure in meeting one who had done so much for the military forces of the country. As regards his business life, Lt-Col May converted John May & Co. into a liability company in which, as chairman, he retained the principal interest.

During his first mayoralty he laid the foundation stone of the Lesser Market and one of the foundation stones of Fairfields Board School. It was no accident that he was mayor during the great celebration years, for as such a great benefactor, he was specifically asked to stand as mayor at those times.

In the Coronation year he paid for banquets at the Town Hall and gave many gifts to the poor. During that mayoralty he also presented an address of welcome to Lord Kitchener on his return from South Africa. On one occasion he entertained 1,650 schoolchildren to tea.

Lt-Col May lived at Hawkfield, just off the Bounty Road, a road named in his honour for the great bounty he had given to Basingstoke. During his first mayoralty May Street, formerly Longcroft, was named after him.

One gift he made during his last few years in Basingstoke was to donate the bells to All Saints' Church, which was built during World War One. He wanted his gift to be unique so he donated nine bells instead of the customary eight.

Lt-Col May moved to Portsmouth toward the end of his very rich life. His body was brought back for burial in the Chapel Hill cemetery.

THE HAYMARKET

W HEN THE decision was taken in 1865 to build a Corn Exchange in the flourishing market town of Basingstoke, no-one had any idea of what the future had in store. Basingstoke would lose its livestock market and agricultural merchants, but the Corn Exchange would remain a great asset even when its use was changed to that of a centre of entertainment.

The old Corn Exchange was eventually to become, firstly, the Grand Cinema and from 1951, the Haymarket, an appropriate name suggested by a Basingstoke GP, Dr H. Radford Potter, which combined its link with farming with the name of a famous London theatre.

The Corn Exchange, opened in 1865. It is now the Haymarket Theatre.

The Haymarket Theatre before refurbishment.

Patience scene with cast of Basingstoke Amateur Operatic Society, 1964.

Very aptly, the opening of the Corn Exchange on 1 March 1865 was celebrated as an important event, giving rise to demonstrations of joy, as recorded in Samuel Attwood's Basingstoke diary:

> A procession approached the town from Hackwood Road and included Lord Bolton, then the owner of Hackwood Park. Four hundred took part in the procession and in the evening two dinners were held, one for the leading townspeople at the Town Hall, followed by a ball which lasted until 4am. Another dinner was held for the ordinary townspeople who wanted to attend.

When the Corn Exchange opened it had no seated accommodation. It was just a hall, with stalls for trading in corn, wheat, barley, and oats. For the retail sale of vegetables, there was the Lesser Market between the Corn Exchange and the Town Hall, with a passageway from Wote Street to Church Street where, in the winter, the poor people of Basingstoke could buy soup for one penny a pint. This was endowed by private subscription.

It was not long before another use was found for the Corn Exchange with its spacious hall. It became a place for public meetings and one of the first VIP's to speak there was General Booth, following the uproar in the town during the Salvation Army riots. It then became a rival of the Feathers Hotel opposite, used by strolling minstrels and the like to entertain. Until 1913 it was used by travelling companies of players and also as a roller-skating rink. From the early days, the rooms below were used to house the town's fire engine, with the horses having to be brought up from the Barge Inn at the bottom of Wote Street.

The real change to the building occurred in 1913 when Mr Casey opened it as a combined variety and cinema house in the days of the silent films. To mark the end of the old Corn Exchange, a new sloping floor and theatre seating was installed, a projection room built and the stage fitted with lighting and scenery. When the building was restored after being gutted by fire in 1925, the columns supporting the roof were removed and the roof reconstructed in one span, the interior being remodelled to conform to that of a theatre.

Mr Casey's occupation continued for several years, during which he used it as a cinema. He named it The Grand, first showing silent black and white films before 'movies' and, eventually, colour films were established.

The Haymarket Theatre.

In the late 1930s, Will Hammer Theatres Ltd took the building over commercially, following a successful run by a repertory company, which ended with the outbreak of war in September 1939. Hammer Theatres' tenancy ended in 1950 when the Basingstoke Borough Council, owners of the building, advertised for tenants. Some offers were received, none of which were thought to be satisfactory. In the meantime, several local people were hoping that the borough council would manage the theatre and so enable the Salisbury Arts Company, which had a very popular following, to continue to visit Basingstoke.

A scheme of management was started as a result of a letter in the *Basingstoke Gazette* – then the *Hants & Berks Gazette* – inviting people to guarantee an annual payment if losses were made and so support the formation of a non-profit making company. The response was astonishing, and in a short time around 100 people guaranteed about £800 per annum for three years. With such backing, a deputation met the borough council representatives to discuss a lease. The council eventually let the theatre to the Basingstoke Theatre Association, which managed it for many years. In each of the first three years, a small loss was made, which was covered by the borough council and the guarantors.

Mr Joice's coach works in Windover Street, which ran north from Winchester Street, before the fire.

Basingstoke's first Town Hall clock. The Corn Exchange, which later became the Haymarket, in the background.

Meanwhile, the Theatre Association were depressed by the gloomy interior of the theatre. Inspired by Mr Frank Lanham, head of a local departmental store and chairman of the Theatre Association, an appeal fund was launched, as a result of which £600 was raised.

For many years, the programme at the Haymarket was chiefly provided by amateur companies with the occasional professional support. The programme ranged from boxing to ballet, pantomime to puppetry, orchestral concerts to Shakespeare. The first large amateur company to perform there was the Thornycroft and Basingstoke Amateur Operatic Society, followed by the Basingstoke Amateur Theatrical Society.

The turning point came when Guy Slater formed the Horseshoe Theatre Company and staged many plays, gaining recognition as the theatre's repertory company. Guy Slater, a very influential actor and producer, negotiated with many leading artistes who subsequently performed at the theatre, including Peter Cushing, Helen Ryan and Timothy West. In addition, well-known personalities such as Cyril Fletcher and Roy Hudd have made appearances at the Haymarket. The

BBC have also made 'live' broadcasts of the popular 'Any Questions' radio programme from the theatre.

Today, the Haymarket Theatre, with many professional plays staged and a wide range of ambitious musicals peformed by local companies, compliments the much larger Anvil Theatre which has three times the seating capacity.

From small beginnings, backed by many thoughtful, optimistic people, and most of all many voluntary workers in the Haymakers' Association, the Haymarket is now one of the leading theatres in Hampshire.

FIRES

WHAT HAS been described as Basingstoke's biggest fire occurred on Monday 17 April 1905 at Winchester Street, when Burberry's department store, the largest in Basingstoke, was destroyed. The fire began at 6pm when one of the shop girls was lighting the gas lamps with a taper in the front window. The material draped about her was highly flammable, and the flames shot across the main shop in what can only be described as a fire-ball. It could have had fatal consequences, for there was a workroom at the back of the store used as a repair shop and the girls working there were lucky to escape with the flames swirling around them.

In those days, the town's steam fire engine was kept beneath the Corn Exchange, with the horses stabled at the bottom of Wote Street. The fire alarm bell hung outside the Town Hall. Some of the firemen were instructed to go to the stables to collect the horses while the rest of the brigade raised steam for the pump on the engine. The brigade made a quick turn-out but, alas, with brigades summoned from Alton and Andover, the pressure of the local mains water supply was so low as to be ineffective. Jets were turned away from the main blaze and played on to the buildings on the opposite side of the road that were in danger of catching fire.

There were other consequences which led to major works being undertaken in the months following the fire, with new water mains being laid of a wider bore. This led to another disaster when, as a result of mains water pipes being inadvertently connected to the sewerage system, a typhoid epidemic broke out with some fatalities.

As the Alton brigade galloped through the avenue at Lasham, one of their horses dropped dead, which obviously caused delay. The Andover brigade actually arrived by rail, their fire appliance being conveyed in a luggage van. The Winchester brigade was also sent for but was forbidden to attend by the City Fathers, who said that they did not pay their fire brigade to fight other town's fires. However, individual

Fire at the Grand Cinema, now the Haymarket, but originally the Corn Exchange, 1925.

Burberry's great fire of 1905, which destroyed much of Winchester Street.

Joice's Yard fire, 1974.

members of the Winchester brigade came to Basingstoke and offered their services.

The fire, which raged for three days, extended to New Street, literally destroying all the departments. Flying embers reached Fairfields School some 300 yards away. There were 27 dressmakers in the workshop under the supervision of their manager, Miss Claridge. Over the store were apartments for 25 women workers and another 20 sleeping in accommodation in Burberry's premises on the other side of the road.

With so many pumps in use, water supply was a problem. The Alton brigade took their steamer to the canal, from where they pumped water through hoses laid in Potters Lane and New Street. The Andover brigade drew their water from the River Loddon, with hoses laid through Church Street, Church Square, Church Lane and New Street.

There was insufficient hose and so additional lengths were borrowed from the London and South Western Railway.

Burberry's workshops, where many tailors and tailoresses were employed making garments popular in many countries of the world, were in Hackwood Road. In later years, the company had a showroom in London Street for the display of riding suits, breeches and so on.

An unfortunate aspect of the fire was that some looting occurred and Basingstoke folk could be seen walking home during the night with goods they had salvaged from the rubble. Later in the night, the captain of the Basingstoke brigade, master tailor Mr Evans, ordered six men from the house of Mr Aldous next door to Burberry's where, he said 'that they were up to no good purpose'. The report in the *Hants & Berks Gazette* said 'he took one or two of them by the neck and forced them from the premises'.

Two commercial companies lucky to escape destruction were Joices' coachworks in Windover Street and John Mare's clothing factory in New Street.

Damage to the premises was assessed at £25,000, which was a considerable sum of money in 1905. All the premises and contents were insured.

Later the shop was bought by Mr Frank Lanham, who owned it for many years. It was later sold to Thomas Wallis. Part of it is now the Chicago Rock Bar.

THORNYCROFT

FROM 1898 until 1972, Thornycroft could claim to be at the heart of the Basingstoke economy, being by far the town's main employer. The company had the reputation, in its prime, of being the 'Rolls-Royce' of the lorry manufacturing industry. Thornycroft lorries were well-respected among commercial vehicles in many parts of the world.

When Sir John I. Thornycroft opened his Basingstoke works after moving the plant from Chiswick in 1898, he was actually experimenting with steam traction for commercial road purposes.

A J-class Thornycroft lorry – many were built for the army during World War One.

However, within a very short time the emphasis was focused on the use of the internal combustion engine and among the early Thornycroft vehicles powered by this means were omnibuses, many of which were built for use in London.

Before priority was given to lorry manufacture, Sir John turned his attention to motor cars. Early photographs of the Worting Road plant show the 'Thornycroft Motor Car Company' painted in large letters on buildings which could be seen by travellers using the main railway line from London to Southampton, Bournemouth, Salisbury and Exeter. Few of the travellers would have known that, but for the decision-making of Basingstoke town council, they would have been looking at a railway works.

Coming toBasingstoke, Sir John I. Thornycroft was a man full of ambition who was content to start from scratch by buying a farm, pasture land and the fine West Ham House, with the area nearest to the town being selected for his works. Sir John Thornycroft, in an early publication, related how on one occasion cash flow was such a problem that he had to sell a hayrick standing outside where the offices were built.

At Chiswick, he traded under the title of the 'Thornycroft Steam Wagon Company Ltd', but within three years the title was changed to that of 'John I. Thornycroft & Co Ltd'. The business was first established at Chiswick in 1864 by the then Mr John Isaac Thornycroft, and within seven years he had caused something of a sensation in the shipbuilding world. The company built a steam launch, *Miranda*, which achieved the unprecedented speed of 18 knots. The shipbuilding section was moved to Woolston, where the Thornycroft name has been carried on as Vosper Thornycroft.

With the coming of the firm to Basingstoke, the west end of the town

Output of Thornycroft lorries, 1915.

Thornycroft output between the wars.

Thornycroft works in the early days – the picture shows that the firm were to build motor cars.

A map of Basingstoke showing Thornycroft's.

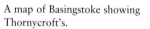

took on a different look when the Brookvale estate was built. Many of the houses accommodated Thornycroft workers, and some houses in George Street were built by the firm for their employees. Record books show the expansion of the firm. In 1904 the wage bill was around £185 a week and during Edwardian days it reached over £375 a week for all those not classified as staff. By 1913 it had reached £900 a week. One member of my family who had emigrated to America, returned to

Basingstoke to work for the firm. A small contingent of Chiswick workers moved with the firm to Basingstoke to make their homes in the town.

World War One took its toll, and thousands of the cream of young British soldiers fell in battle. The armies had to be maintained and equipped and this meant much advancement in business for engineering firms, including Thornycroft.

The company was contracted to build thousands of lorries for the Army, the most famous being the 'J' type. In addition, many guns were built and for years after the Armistice, a number of Thornycroft-made guns could be seen among the trees at West Ham Park. The park included football pitches and a large stand, as well as two cricket pitches, a hockey pitch, two tennis courts and a bowling green. A popular addition was a licensed club house where competitive darts was played. The company built a fine, well-equipped canteen, with a stage where the Thornycroft Amateur Operatic Society produced most of the Gilbert and Sullivan operas. With many musicians among the staff, including a number of former bandsmen, the company had its own band from which musicians were extracted to form an orchestra for the light opera performances.

Thornycroft's was the first Basingstoke company to bring in women employees to do work usually reserved for men. This was in order to

Depth-charge throwers built at Thornycroft's.

Women workers at Thornycroft's during World War One.

A Thornycroft-built 1914–1918 gun, now in the Imperial War Museum.

Interior shot of the Thornycroft works.

fill the gaps caused by men serving with the forces. The women had to wear mob caps for safety after one female employee had her hair caught up in a pillar drill and was scalped.

During the 1920s and 1930s a large variety of lorries were built, many for overseas. The company had agencies and workshops in Australia, South America and other countries. The chassis were secured in large packing cases and the bodies built overseas.

Like industry in general, the works went through a slack period, with some workers moving on to car factories at Luton. Each morning, a number of unemployed men would gather outside the gatehouse hoping to catch the eye of the Personnel Manager, Mr Pat Chandler. In the 1930s work picked up and for some years, men in the machine-shop in particular would be asked to return to work after a brief respite for tea on a Friday and work through the night until Saturday morning. This was accelerated when orders from the Ministry of Defence came flocking in as the international scene deteriorated in 1938–1939.

When the war broke out in September 1939 the works were all geared up to provide military equipment, in addition to maintaining

production of lorries for the home market. Thornycroft's was chosen to build thousands of Bren gun carriers and searchlight lorries. As the war developed, 7 and 17-pounder guns were built. This meant sacrificing the football pitch and stand for a building for gun manufacturing. Among the male operatives were a number of women. A night-shift was started before war was declared and this continued into peacetime. The labour force was increased drastically, topping 2,000. Even today, there are very few old Basingstoke families without one or two relatives who have worked for the company.

There were many highly skilled workmen in Thornycroft's during the war and it is significant that the company was chosen to build the first three amphibian vehicles, known as 'Terrapins' or 'Ducks'. The drawings for the prototype were received in November 1942, and within six weeks they were complete and handed over to the Ministry for trials. They were required for the invasion of Normandy in June 1944, 18 months after the prototypes were built. Deemed successful,

Presentation to Mr Tom Thornycroft in 1934, on the occasion of his second wedding.

Buses produced by John I. Thornycroft and Co. Ltd, photographed at the works.

Teams representing Thornycroft staff and works, before World War One.

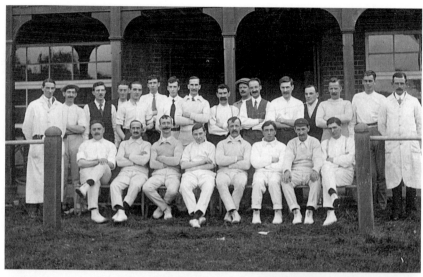

A row of Antars at the works awaiting delivery.

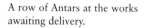

The Terrapin amphibious landing craft – the first three made at Thornycroft's.

orders were placed with Morris-Cowley in Oxford for the 'Terrapins' to be mass-produced.

As the panel shows, other quantities of military equipment were produced. A widely used Thornycroft lorry was the 'Amazon' type, many of which were equipped with a Coles crane for use by the Royal Air Force for aircraft recovery.

After the war, Thornycroft's developed a name for building one of the largest lorries to use British roads – the 'Mighty Antar'. Built primarily as a tank transporter and powered by a petrol engine, its unladen fuel capacity was two miles per gallon. Another large vehicle was the 'Big Ben' type, many being supplied to the Middle East for use in laying oil pipelines.

WARTIME ACHIEVEMENTS 1939 - 1945

Thornycroft became one of the most important suppliers of vehicles, ships and engineering equipment for the second world war. A summary of the equipment delivered to the forces, from the Basingstoke Plant, is listed below:

13,000 Military wheeled vehicles - types included were:

"AMAZON"	Coles Cranes vehicles.
"STURDY"	Searchlight lorries.
"STURDY"	General service lorries, including tippers for aerodrome construction and repair, RAF mobile power units and water carriers
"TF NUBIAN"	4x4, similar chassis to the fire engine you see exhibited by The Thornycroft Society today.
"WO"/"WOF"	Used as general load carriers, workshop lorries, war dept survey lorries, photographic and wireless vehicles.

8,230   Bren Gun Carriers

1,850   Sets of Flotation Gear for the above, to cross canals/rivers under their own power

15,000 Sets of torpedo rudders for 18" and 21" aerial and underwater torpedo's.

11,000 Connecting rods for Paxman Ricardo Engines for tank landing craft.

5,637   Balance weights for Bristol Aero Engines.

670   Sets of 2 PDR Guns

1760   Sets of 17 PDR Guns

Together with many thousands of breech rings, blocks and firing mechanisms, also parts for Rolls Royce and Napier Aero engines, exploders for 4,000 pound bombs, gun barrels, other parts for O.S.B. 3" Mk I Gun.
Depth Charge throwers.
Responsibility for the design/manufacture of prototype Amphibious Terrapin I, then manufacture was handed over to Morris Commercial Cars Ltd, Birmingham as the Basingstoke plant was occupied to capacity, later a Mk II version was designed.

* A further 2,000 vehicles for civilian use were also built during the 1939-1945 war period.

Thornycroft production at the Basingstoke works during World War Two.

Thornycroft workforce.

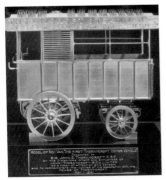

The pioneer steam wagon built at Thornycroft's in around 1899.

The 1,000th Bren gun carrier built at Thornycroft's during World War Two.

The Thornycroft football team, headed by Doug Gittens, leaving their club house.

Gradually, competition in the commercial vehicle market became acute and Thornycroft's was plagued by a shortage of labour. Many of the skilled workforce left to take employment with other engineering companies in the vicinity. A trading arrangement was made with two competitors, Scammell's and AEC, but the demise of the Thornycroft company was inevitable, and the last Thornycroft chassis left the shops in 1972.

Engineering continued for some more years with the machine-shop and one or two other departments being taken over by Eaton's Transmission, an American company with British headquarters in Manchester. Hundreds of gear-boxes were manufactured until the closure of Eaton's in the 1980s. For some years the plant lay idle until the site was purchased by Safeway for a supermarket. Many a tear was shed by former Thornycroft workers as they saw the empty and silent workshops where some had spent most of their working lives. It was hard to bear when the time came for the factory to be reduced to piles of bricks and tangled girders. During the last 25 years, West Ham Park, with its luscious trees and greensward, was acquired for redevelopment.

Today the Thornycroft Society has over 200 members, mainly made up of owners of vintage Thornycroft vehicles and former employees.

Reminders of the old company remain with two cranes. One is outside the Safeway petrol station, and the other, a huge travelling overhead crane from one of the workshops, which has been preserved in working order, can be seen in the Thornycroft section of the new Milestones Museum, built quite near to where the Thornycroft plant stood.

CHRISTMAS IN THE 1920s

L IKE EVERY other aspect of life, Christmas has changed over the years and I am fortunate to have a good memory which brings back so clearly the Christmases of the 1920s. In that decade, I grew from a four-year-old boy to a youth of 14. One exciting activity was to prepare to decorate the house with paper chains. I remember going with my sister Doris to Whiteman's shop, latterly Nutt's, in Church Street, to buy packs of coloured paper strips and a bottle of gum. What contented hours we had making the paper chains and then hanging them up round the rooms.

Of course, goodies help to make the festive season more exciting. I looked forward to the day when my Uncle Arthur and Aunty Emmy, who had a large bakery business at Slough, visited us. One of their specialities was fancy cakes, and when I heard the noise of the engine of Uncle Arthur's powerful Indian motor-cycle and combination, my eyes bulged as I saw the cakes, chocolates and sweets being unloaded. I am sure that some of these found their way into my stocking.

The stocking I had was a discarded one and not one of the gaudy kind. What surprising things I unravelled – pink mice made of sugar, apples and oranges and small items such as miniature games, even coal! In those days, we had no recorded music and so my father might give us a tune on his whistle pipe.

Apart from Brook Street School, where I lost much time through illness, my outside interests were chiefly playing with those of my age in the street. I could never remember who started what, there were marbles, leap-frog up the centre of the street, trolling hoops, spinning tops, hop-scotch, tip-it and even skipping. When one amusement faded out, along came another.

It was possible to play in the road or on the pavement, for to see a car was a rarity. Parents did not worry about children playing outside or at King George's playing field nearby, for attacks on children were very seldom heard of.

As for getting into trouble, we children were afraid of policemen, and there was a police house close to my home. I remember PC Page, Sergeant Keel and most of all, Constable Shelley.

What gave me much pleasure as a barely 12-year-old was to join St Michael's Choir. This was in 1928 when I commenced continuous membership, which I am still enjoying after 73 years service.

There are many men in Basingstoke who have never forgotten their days as choirboys. We averaged 20 and they came from all walks of life, but the best boys seemed to be the sons of publicans! Among these were boys from the Self Defence and the Black Boy. During Advent, we would practice carols but were not permitted to sing them in church until Christmas Day. In those days, however, many boys and girls toured the streets knocking doors to collect pocket money by virtue of their singing. The other reminder of the approach of Christmas was provided by the Salvation Army, and not one street in the town would be missed.

On the great day, we choirboys were expected to sing at the children's service at 10am, Matins at 11am and in the afternoon we sang in the various wards of the Hackwood Road Hospital. Afterwards, we were entertained to tea.

My choirmaster and organist was Mr Syd Anstey, a blind man who lost his sight through measles when he was 17. His first post was at Haverfordwest, Wales and he must have been appointed to St Michael's in 1920 where he remained in the post for 50 years. Apart from being a brilliant organist, he was also an organ repairer as well as teaching the organ and pianoforte. Despite his disability, he would visit country churches to play at services and undertake repairs.

Choir practice was held in the main hall of St John's School where Mrs Anstey would always be present to keep the boys in order. Every year there would be a choir outing to Portsmouth, Bournemouth or the Isle of Wight, where, while the boys were having fun on the beach, Mrs Anstey was to be seen in the centre of a great heap of clothing, and bags, which she was looking after.

I am afraid the boys of my time rather played up Mr and Mrs Anstey and sometimes suprised the school's caretaker by taking refuge in the cellars. Many boys arrived home from choir practice for their parents to ask why were they so dirty? They had been hiding among the piles of coal in order to escape the wrath of Mrs Anstey!

On New Year's Eve, there was a nightwatch service at St Michael's. At 11.50pm the choir would ascend the tower to sing the hymn *All People That On Earth Do Dwell* after the church clock had struck midnight. Invariably, after the hymn had been sung, a different kind of singing would emanate from the Square below, where those who had left the pubs would gather. The practice of ascending the tower ended after Canon Boustead retired in 1936 and was succeeded by the Venerable Anthony Chute. Churchgoing in those days was much more popular than today with many of the services being packed, the church in those days holding 800 people.

One attraction every Christmas was the Christmas Forest at St John's School, when Christmas trees would line the hall on which presents were hung, a ticket buying a child or parent a gift.

The shops in the town looked a picture, with legs of beef and lamb hanging on hooks outside butchers' shops, sometimes the head of an ox, plus numerous pheasants, partridges, chickens, ducks and a few turkeys. The beef, lamb and pork would have come from animals sold at the Christmas Fat Stock Show at the Cattle Market outside the railway station.

The cost of living in those days was comparatively low, and coal was brought round to the houses at 2s 7d a hundredweight. The town used to have its old characters, for example 'Happy Bob', who traded in fruit and winkles from his truck outside the Barge Inn at the bottom of Wote Street.

How the social order has changed. As a journalist, I have covered golden and diamond weddings and been told how the bridegroom would be given the morning off but had to return to work in the afternoon. I was told by one man, who worked at a butcher's shop, that he was only given Christmas Day off to get married and that he had to return on Boxing Day to prepare the shop for opening on the following day. He was told that if he did not turn up he would be sacked. He reported for work early on the morning of 27 December and was promptly dismissed.

At Thornycroft's, work would continue until 5.30pm on Christmas Eve and restart on the day after Boxing Day, but such demands on the employees were gradually relaxed in the late 1930s.

One event which characterised every Christmas was the traditional meeting of the Vine Hunt on Boxing Day morning. The hunt gathered in the yard of the Wheatsheaf Inn and moved off from the Market Place. Usually, the hunt, often with the mayor mounted, would proceed in the London Road direction. Many riders turned out in their hunting scarlet, with members of the public following if they had transport. The electrification of the railway in the 1960s terminated this annual event and thus ended a tradition going back many years.

By the time my voice broke, we had music at home in the form of a gramophone, and within a year, a one-valve radio set. I have to say that I found the music programmes, often consisting of popular classics, more interesting than many of today's TV programmes.

Wages were low, and many wives of the working classes, with the exception of those who were tailoresses at Burberry's, John Mare's or Gerrish, Ames and Simpkins', often looked for some charring. The other great difference from today was that middle-class families, such as those of doctors, dentists, clergy, solicitors and top businessmen, invariably employed one, two or even three maids.

Although money was hard to come by, these were happy days when many artisans took an allotment which gave them much pleasure and provided fresh vegetables. A number of allotment holders kept chicken and pigs, many of which would die as Christmas approached.

EVENTS AND ENTERTAINMENT

The carnival queen about to move off in the annual carnival procession.

THE ENTERTAINMENT scene really took off during the post-war years, and continued to thrive as there was a great influx of population from the 1960s onwards. Arts organisations were formed, not only to provide fun for the players, but entertainment for the local masses.

The Thornycroft Amateur Operatic Society, founded in 1922, ceased productions after less than 10 years, although their interpretations of the Savoy operas in the Thornycroft canteen were very popular. At the end of World War Two, a few enthusiasts in the Thornycroft works re-founded the society, which went from strength to strength, moving its productions to the Haymarket Theatre in 1951, the Festival of Britain year. Initially, the society concentrated their productions on the Gilbert and Sullivan light operas, but in later years musicals such as *Annie Get Your Gun*, *Pink Champagne* and the ever popular *The Merry Widow*

The Coronation float of the Basingstoke Amateur Operatic Society in the Coronation procession of 1953.

Opening of pavilion at May's Bounty cricket ground.

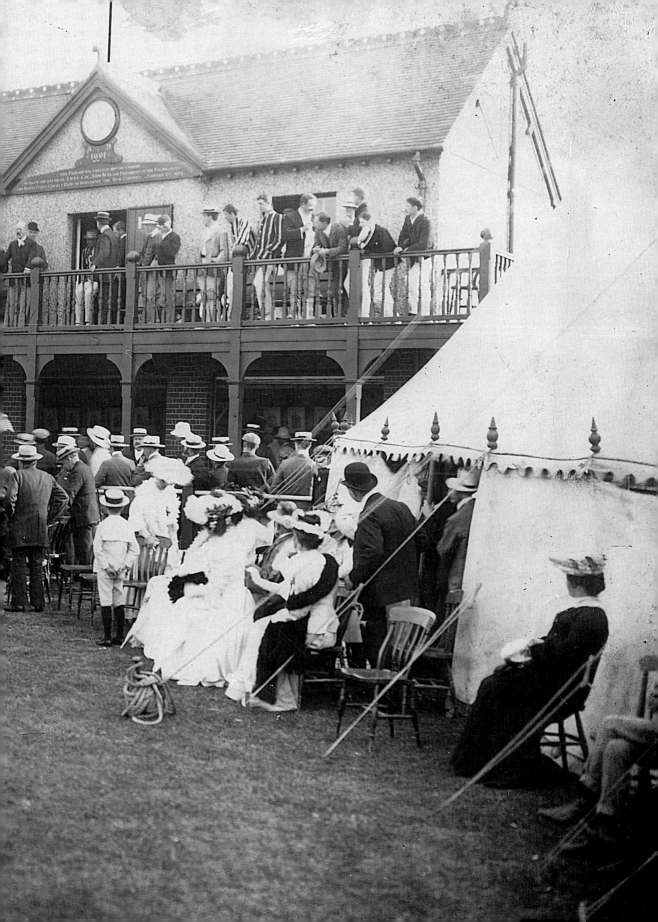

The Basingstoke male voice choir appearing on one of their American tours.

were staged. The Haymarket Theatre would normally be full for the eight performances.

In the 1960s, another company was formed called the Basingstoke Amateur Theatrical Society, now known as the BATS. They scored great success in staging American musicals and above all, an annual pantomime which was so popular that it would fill the Haymarket Theatre night after night. The general local opinion was that the standard of these popular shows was superior to those produced on the London stage.

With many newcomers longing for good entertainment, backed by enthusiastic locals, the Basingstoke Male Voice Choir was formed. From a modest beginning, the choir became 80 strong and carried the name of Basingstoke far and wide. After successes at Eisteddfods in Wales, tours were undertaken in America, Canada, Germany and Holland as well as to many centres in Great Britain. Today, they are so popular that they can fill the 1,500 seats at the Haymarket Theatre.

Another choir which began in a small way is the Basingstoke Ladies Choir, founded by a group of keen housewives on the Oakridge estate – an estate built originally for employees of the Atomic Weapons Research Establishment at Aldermaston. Originally the Oakridge Singers, they rightly changed their name to the Basingstoke Ladies

Choir. They have appeared at the Anvil, but of late have been using the Haymarket Theatre where their annual concerts have often been held. They too have travelled widely, visiting Canada, France and Germany. These amateur organisations have excelled in supplementing entertainments by the professionals and at the same time have catered for many who have looked for ways in which to fulfil ambitions of being participators in the arts.

Basingstoke is very well endowed with music lovers, both orchestral players and singers. The Basingstoke Symphony Orchestra, which gives three concerts a year at the Anvil, has a reputation second to none for its high standard of playing. Many works are included in their programmes which few amateur orchestras could tackle. Top artistes are often engaged as soloists and among the audience are many music lovers from London and the suburbs.

The Basingstoke Choral Society, with a chorus 100 strong, has a splendid following and sings the most difficult choral works. Apart from their Anvil appearances, the society gives well-attended concerts

Church Street showing the
Coronation decorations.

in Winchester Cathedral. Their performances are often supported by some of the best singers in the country, including Elizabeth Garrett.

The Anvil is looked upon as one of the finest concert halls in England with acoustics rarely to be found. Many leading performers appear, including comedians, top pop groups, professional pantomimes and some of the leading professional orchestras including the Bournemouth Symphony Orchestra and the Mozart Players.

The Anvil, which was opened during the last decade of the 20th century, was built on an open space, originally part of the site of the John May & Company's brewery. This stupendous venture was only made possible by financial support from the Basingstoke and Deane Borough Council, the Hampshire County Council and the Arts Council. The hope that such a venture could be successful has been more than justified and now has a great following.

Built alongside Churchill Way and within a few yards of Basingstoke Railway Station, the Anvil has a fine bar and dining facilities open to patrons and visitors in the daytime. The construction is ultra-modern and has an auditorium with seating that can be lowered beneath floor-level to make a dance floor and banqueting hall.

Car parking is adequate with a large area of the town parking system adjoining the hall and further parking by Glebe Gardens. The Anvil is a most appropriate name for the hall as some 500 yards to the east was

The open-air swimming pool at West Ham.

the works of Wallis & Steevens, road roller manufacturers, who had a forge at the bottom of the town on a level with the Anvil.

St Michael's Church is very well known for its highly esteemed church choir which has been in existence from late Victorian days. It is one of the top Anglican choirs in the diocese of Winchester, and has sung in the cathedral on many occasions. The singers are drawn from a wide area, many from outside the parish.

Entertainment, from the days of the strolling singers and mummers through to the present time, not forgetting the concerts given by several brass bands, has been an important part in the life of the population and is still well supported despite the competition of television. Local entertainment must have a part in the town's history.

People often wonder how our ancestors amused themselves before the days of radio and television, apart from visiting inns when work was done to indulge in gossip rather than drinking. On days of national rejoicing, few people would miss the fun by staying at home. Basingstoke had two Fair Days a year, when parents and children alike

Lower Brook Street Coronation street party in 1953, attended by Alderman and Mrs John Stroud.

would turn out in their hundreds and go to Sam Stoke's fairground, off what is now Victory Roundabout, or visit Whittle's amusements at the Wheatsheaf Meadow, Sarum Hill. Earlier last century, much fascination was to be had from the great showmens' steam engines, rocking on their wheels generating electricity to power the cakewalk, chairoplanes,

Queen's walkabout, 1972. She is seen chatting with the pearly king.

The Town Hall illuminated with gas for the 1902 celebrations.

roundabouts and side-stalls and to light up all the coloured bulbs on the rides and side-shows.

Lots of people, especially those unable to climb the helter-skelter or to be dashed around on the whip, found great fun in trying their luck on the aeroplanes, hoping that their card would be with the winner. The prizes made a glittering display, with large stuffed toys, clocks, canteens of cutlery and many other much sought after articles.

These fairs cheered up many a dull autumn evening. There were the oddest of side-shows, including a woman with three arms, the tiniest dwarves imaginable, rifle ranges, darts and coconut shies. For the

ELBY and SON, OUTFITTERS.

Basingstoke
Market
Square.

Scouts often visited Lasham. Here is a glider with Laurie Bittlestone, a former Scouter, at the controls with Mayoress Mrs Jackson.

children, great excitement would be caused when traction engines and vintage lorries arrived in the town, drawing the various amusements.

Today the fairs are no longer associated with the carnivals, which are now a thing of the past, and do not seem to engender the same excitement.

Many people regret the passing of the annual carnival, the last of which took place in the 1990s. The procession in Basingstoke was one of the biggest in Hampshire, attracting many entries from employees of the many new firms which have moved

The bandstand in the Council Road recreation ground, which is now in War Memorial Park.

A royal visit to Basingstoke by the Duke of Gloucester, who went to the Boys' Club at the old Silk Mill near Victory Square.

A gymnastic display at the rectory garden party.

to Basingstoke, mostly from the London area. The decorative tableaux were beautifully conceived. The choosing of the Carnival Queen by an election arranged by the *Basingstoke Gazette* was democracy at its very best. Thousands of people lined the streets to watch the procession which could take two hours to pass. The children had their separate processions and a junior queen with attendants. Many of the newcomers from London could have hardly experienced such fun-days, with the opportunity to participate in them.

Other great days still remembered by many people are those of the street parties marking the peace celebrations, coronations and silver jubilees.

These days of celebrations could never happened but for the willingness of people to join together to make costumes or to decorate streets and buildings. It was the demonstration of community which led to many new friends being made and, above all, was achieved with very little rowdyism. They have been very much a part of Basingstoke's history.

EDUCATION

BASINGSTOKE is lucky to have fine provision for education. It has a sixth form college from where many students have proceeded to institutions of higher education. Also, Basingstoke College of Technology (BCOT) provides educational opportunities in a wide range of subjects, catering for both full-time and part-time students from a wide area of North Hampshire. The college, which has been enlarged during the past five years, at one time occupied the building in which Queen Mary's Grammar School was situated. Sadly, this building was demolished some years ago to make way for new college facilities. One of the features of BCOT is the Newman Restaurant, where catering students receive training in the preparation and serving of fine meals, which are available to members of the public. The restaurant is named after Mr R.F. Newman, who was for many years managing director of Thornycroft's and an original governor of the college. Mr Newman initiated the BCOT by transferring the Thornycroft apprentice school to the old grammar school building.

The college's main building was built at Worting Road on a high bank

Technical college students celebrate rag day in the 1950s.

Fairfields School, Basingstoke, 1935. The Winchester Festival choir.

occupying a former allotments site. Formerly known as Basingstoke Technical College, BCOT is considered by many people to be an educational institution that is likely to receive university status in years to come.

The boys' grammar school occupied the site opposite the main BCOT building for many years. Originally in the grounds of the Holy Ghost cemetery (Liten), the school moved shortly before World War Two to a site in Vyne Road. When secondary education was reorganised in Basingstoke during 1972, Queen Mary's ceased to be a selective grammar school and merged with the adjacent Charles Chute

A presentation at Queen Mary's School by Councillor Jack Welling, the mayor. Mrs Welling was also present.

Fairfield's School showing high grass growing opposite – a flashback to the days of the sheep fairs.

Secondary Modern School for Boys to become a comprehensive co-educational school. It was renamed The Vyne School.

The Charles Chute Secondary Modern School for Boys was named after Sir Charles Chute who, at one time, was chairman of Hampshire County Council. Opened in 1960, the school had a comparatively short life as a secondary modern school. The school buildings had a short life too, as they were demolished in the 1990s to make way for a housing development.

With Queen Mary's Grammar School linked to the Guild of the Holy Ghost, transferring to the Worting Road site in 1855 and with no complementary girls' grammar school, boys in Victorian days had the advantage over girls. This was rectified in the early days of the last century when a girls' grammar school was opened at Brook House, to be transferred a few years later to new buildings at Crossborough Hill. Known as Basingstoke High School for Girls, the first Headmistress was Miss Harriet Costello. The school, on a site adjoining Basingstoke Common, narrowly escaped destruction during World War Two when it was deluged with incendiary bombs, which fire-watchers did well to extinguish. The school became a co-educational comprehensive when secondary education was reorganised in 1972 and was renamed The Harriet Costello School.

Queen Mary's College has occupied the former Shrubbery Secondary Modern School for Girls site in Cliddesden Road since 1972 and is the sixth form college for the Basingstoke area. There have been additions to the original Shrubbery School buildings of 1954 over the years and the college has a fine academic record.

Perhaps the greatest step in the town's education provision was the building of Fairfields Board School in 1887. Built on lush fields to the south of Basingstoke town centre, the school was so named because it occupied the site where, for many years, sheep fairs were held.

St John's School, Church Street, now demolished.

The Harriet Costello School Orchestra, conducted by Miss Mason.

The school building housed boys on the ground floor and girls on the upper storey, and had an annexe where a primary school was situated. The first scholars came from the British School in Sarum Hill and the independent girls' school in Cross Street. Mr George Gage, a prominent Basingstoke man, was transferred from the headship of the British School to become the first headmaster of Fairfields.

The school, with its high tower, is one of Basingstoke's landmarks. It was built by Mr Goodall of Worting, a very small builder, whose estimate was accepted. Mr Goodall was an enterprising man, prepared to attempt anything. For a time before he became a builder and constructed Fairfields he was a publican, and he once nearly drowned when his taste for adventure nearly went too far.

Mr Goodall decided that a future could be in store for him in Canada

St John's School.

Queen Mary's School, Worting Road – later demolished to make way for BCOT

so he decided to emigrate. Unfortunately, before reaching harbour, the boat on which he was a passenger was swept on to rocks. Fortunately, he was one of the passengers to be rescued and having lost all of his belongings, he decided to abandon the idea of emigration and return to Basingstoke, where he made a name for himself by erecting what was, at the time, the town's biggest building.

The next school to be built was St John's, situated at the bottom of Church Street. When built, it was an all-age, mixed school and occupied the site of a farm where, many years previously, St John's Hospital had been built by Walter de Merton, founder of Merton College, Oxford.

St John's School catered for children aged from five to 14 and its existence only came about because the vicar of the day, Dr Cooper Smith, needed more accommodation for his Sunday School children. When building work had been completed, he realised that the school building was large enough to accommodate a day school, for which there was a pressing need. Many children, mainly from the north and east of the town, attended the school, which was church-controlled. Part of the boys' playground was actually built over the River Loddon. All went well until the town development plan of the 1960s, when the

school site was required and became the subject of a compulsory purchase order. A replacement building was constructed at Kingsmill Road on the south side of the town and was named St John's Church of England (Aided) School. Infants were taught in a new building nearby with St John's School accommodating junior schoolchildren only. However, within a comparatively short period, these infants were transferred to the St John's School site.

One school, currently being converted into apartments, was Brook Street School, built in 1909 and later known as Brookvale School. Until the 1920s it catered for children from five to 14 years of age, but it then became a primary school, the older pupils transferring to Fairfields School. The school's catchment area was mainly from the area now known as Brookvale.

The development of Basingstoke, mainly in the 1960s and 1970s, required the building of many new schools. However, with the decline in the school population several schools have been closed in recent years at Popley, South View and South Ham. The last school to be built catered for children at Hatch Warren on the southern outskirts of the town.

WAR AND AIR RAIDS

COMPARED WITH many towns and cities, Basingstoke had comparatively few air raids. However, the town did not escape completely, with one raid on the centre of the town on 16 August 1940 claiming nine lives.

Many local people simply could not believe that the war had arrived in the quiet market town, but when it did, it was a shattering experience. The German planes struck at 5.30pm on a Friday when many workpeople were returning home from their shops and factories.

A formation of 12 three-engined bombers flew in from the south over Farleigh Hill when I was still asleep after a gruelling night's work

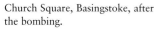
Church Square, Basingstoke, after the bombing.

and about an hour before I was due to rise. My wife heard the noise of approaching aircraft and looked out of the front widow just in time to see the bombs, glistening in the sunlight, leaving the planes. She made a dash up the stairs to rouse me but before getting to the bedroom, our house was shaken although we were about half a mile from where the bombs exploded. As a member of the Home Guard, I donned my uniform and dashed to the bombed area, only to be told to return home.

At around three in the morning, an explosion shook the Thornycroft factory. We all dashed for the shelters quite needlessly, for it was a delayed-action bomb that had exploded.

A stick of bombs fell in the Church Square area where six people were killed, and another dropped about 500 yards north of the town centre in Burgess Road, a pleasant residential area, killing three people. One of the bombs fell in Church Lane killing four people; another landed in Church Street between St Michael's Church and the Methodist Church. When it landed, a motor-cycle combination was passing. The driver, Basingstoke house decorator Mr Lewis Doman, was killed, but his side-car passenger escaped with a mere graze.

A damaged house at the end of Southend Road during a 1941 air raid.

Demolition of the Church Street Methodist Church.

St Michael's Church windows after the air raid of 16 August 1940.

Approaching the spot on the pavement was 20-year-old Joan Stovell, daughter of a Basingstoke music shopkeeper. She died in the blast.

Those killed in Burgess Road were Charles and Ruth Dickson, residents of Winchester Road, and their seven-year-old daughter Angela. They had gone to Burgess Road to see if Mrs Dickson's parents' house was safe as her parents were away.

The damage to the Methodist Church was so great that it had to be rebuilt. The organ, situated well away from the blast, was reduced to a tangled mass of wreckage. St Michael's Church lost all of its glass except for one window at the far end of the church. Most of the windows were completely blown out and among the glass destroyed was a window full of mediaeval glass that had been removed from the ruins of the Holy Ghost Chapel. It was some weeks before St Michael's Church could be used. One of its fine pillars has a scar caused by a piece of flying shrapnel. In Church Square, several fine Georgian houses occupied by doctors and dentists were completely destroyed.

It is believed that five of the 10 attacking aircraft were shot down before they reached the coast on their return journey.

Sad as the consequences of air raids were, there was always the humorous side. At the time, there were farms almost to the perimeter of the town and on what is now the site of Lansing Linde's factory,

The Memorial Garden in Church Square, prepared on the bomb site.

harvesting was in progress in Mr Horton's fields. When the enemy aircraft were approaching, the farm workers were building a hayrick. They buried themselves in the hay and after the explosions found that they could not get down from the

Air raid damage at Solby's Road.

rick as the farm horses, in their panic, had knocked their ladder to the ground. They had to wait until help arrived before they could get down.

The town also suffered a daylight raid when a single enemy aircraft dropped bombs in a residential area close to my home, luckily without any casualties. One bomb, which did not explode, buried itself under a row of terrace houses in May Street and was later successfully made safe and removed by bomb disposal personnel. Later that day, in the early evening, another lone enemy bomber dropped a stick of bombs, one of which landed on a house in Penrith Road, blowing out doors and windows. Another bomb landed on the rectory lawn, showering the rectory with mud and grass.

In another daylight raid, a single enemy aircraft dropped a bomb which destroyed a detached house in Cliddesden Road which was being used as a private school. Luckily, the children were at exercise in the nearby Goldings Park. Two maids were in the building at the time but escaped with injuries. When the rescue party reached one of them, all she asked for was her knickers, which had disappeared! They were seen

One of the two mortuary chapels which were in the Vyne Road Cemetery.

War Bond celebrations in 1917, with a World War One bomber over Winchester Street.

Sir Harold Gillies, a famous plastic surgeon based at Rooksdown Hospital. He was nationally known for his pioneering work rebuilding the faces of servicemen who had been disfigured during World War Two.

later that evening hanging from a branch of an apple tree in the garden of a house further up the road.

Another humourous event occurred after the siren had sounded to give warning of the town centre raid. A fireman jumped on his bike opposite All Saints' Church to make the downhill journey to the fire-station. When passing the two churches in Church Street, he noticed the road was wet but did not know that it was not a puddle, but a bomb crater flooded by a broken water main. He and his bike plunged in, emerging dripping wet. When greeted by a surprised fire chief at the fire-station, he was asked to explain what had happened. All he could say was 'I know where a bomb has dropped'.

HOME GUARD

THE TELEVISION programme *Dad's Army* is very popular, and when I speak in schools about World War Two and mention the Home Guard, children often ask 'Were you in Dad's Army'?

As one working in engineering on work of national importance I was one of thousands who answered the call to enrol in the LDV – the Local Defence Volunteers. This was at the time when things looked very black, with the German Army already in control of many of the channel ports. Everyone wondered whether the Germans, supported by the Luftwaffe, could breach our meagre defences and invade Great Britain.

We in the LDV were enrolled to defend our country and its people. At first we had no proper uniform, only suits of thin denim material and hardly any forage caps. Most importantly, we had no rifles. We had to

The night-shift platoon of the Thornycroft Home Guard – the author is one of the cap-less men.

Anti-tank blocks off Sarum Hill.

drill with imitation rifles cut from wood and play a waiting game until a shipment of .300 rifles arrived from Canada, which meant we could not use the standard .303 ammunition. We were lucky to be issued with a few machine-guns and it fell to me to be given two stripes and become a Lewis gun instructor.

Those early months, when Winston Churchill changed the title of the LDV to the Home Guard, were the most dangerous ones, for the Battle of Britain took place as German aircraft flew over Basingstoke nightly, heading for such places as Birmingham, Coventry and Manchester. Nearer to home, we could see the fires burning at Portsmouth, Southampton and even London, the Blitz being between 25 and 50 miles away.

Working as a Home Guard on the night shift meant going to work with a rifle, respirator, steel helmet and 10 rounds of ammunition. During that summer, interruptions to our work were frequent. When the danger lights came up, we rushed for the shelters.

My unit was the Thornycroft Company of the Home Guard, consisting of eight platoons, each led by an officer with regular army experience and some former soldiers of World War One. Many businessmen served in the Basingstoke Town Company, and the railway also had a company, as did Smith's Industries.

As a member of the night shift, I worked from 8pm to 8am, sometimes six nights a week with the seventh night every three weeks back to the factory on guard duty. Two mornings a week, after tea and toast in the works canteen, we were required to do two hours of field

exercises at South Ham to the west of the works before the area was taken for a housing estate.

Quite often during the night hours, the Home Guard was called out when lights had been reported, thought to be transmitting signals to German aircraft flying overhead. On one occasion, a motor-cyclist entered the area we were guarding and failed to stop. One section was ordered to fire, luckily the shots passed over the man's head. The incident very much disturbed the night's rest of people living in the Brookvale area.

There were one or two amusing happenings, one in particular being very embarrassing for me. One winter's night, when it was so dark I had difficulty in walking on the pavement, I was greeted with howls of laughter as I entered the machine-shop for, on leaving my home with my rifle slung over my shoulder, I had hooked my wife's petticoat off the airing line in the kitchen. I arrived looking as if I was carrying a white flag.

One Saturday night, during a social in the works canteen, I was called out to do anti-looting duty in Penrith Road, which had been bombed in

World War One soldiers in Winton Square.

The World War One tank which stood outside Fairfields' School for many years.

the afternoon. The reason for such a call-out was that several weeks previously, Solby's Road had been bombed, and some of the houses looted. I was ashamed that people in my home town could act in such a way.

We were given every opportunity to take part in exercises, one of which I remember was riding in a Bren gun carrier from Sherborne St John to attack the works which was being defended by the day-shift. The attackers were deemed to have taken the honours, but it was no thanks to me. I was stranded at the top of a fire-escape, being peppered by day-shift men from below.

One incident during training that I remember vividly was when one of my colleagues, who was very short, could not clear the parapet with his grenade. It fell back at his feet. Luckily, the sergeant was there to hustle him into the safety area just in time. Another experience which Home Guard men had in my area was to go to Bisley to practice on the firing-ranges.

One exercise I much enjoyed, when the crops had been reaped, was to take men out on map-reading exercises on Sunday mornings. With the compass we were issued with, it was very rewarding when, by taking readings, we arrived bang on our correct location. As regards the Lewis gun, we had very few chances to fire it because of the scarcity of ammunition. Toward the end of the Home Guard, we were issued with sten guns. We were disbanded months before VE Day, when it became clear that the Germans were not able to land in Britain. The danger then was from V1 and V2 rockets. A V1 landed to the rear of Thornycroft's sports field but caused no casualties.

One experience I had in the Home Guard was to undertake escort duties at a court martial. The prisoner was a very short private from Portsmouth, who had absented himself from Sunday parades. To attend these, he would have had to stay in Basingstoke over the weekend. He was severely reprimanded by the presiding brigadier, and told that should it occur again, he would be sent to prison.

On reflection, the Home Guard could give much pleasure with a chance to see something of the countryside after many hours cooped up in a factory. But, like many others who served in 'Dad's Army', I cannot help thinking what would have happened if we had been called upon to tackle parachutists or, worse still, dash out as the Panzers passed by, to place a sticky-bomb on the side of a tank!

Women's roles altered during World War One. Here a woman does the rounds for the Basingstoke Co-operative Society.

FLOODS

INCREASINGLY, various parts of Great Britain have been stricken with floods, mostly in areas close to rivers. The River Loddon rises in Basingstoke and it may seem quite surprising that this mere trickle of a river has, for many years, caused flooding.

Problems are now being caused by flooding at the Victory roundabout, where the water-table is so high that the underpasses are often impassble, as the spring water is so close to the surface. Unless two pumps are continually in action, residents from the Brookvale and Winklebury areas have great difficulty reaching the town centre or the railway station.

The Victory roundabout, underneath which the River Loddon flows, was named Noah's Island in Victorian days and that was the address given to several cottages just off the road. Brook Street, which leads from Noah's Island, was known as Frog Lane. When the piling required for the construction of the new town centre commenced, pumps which had existed for 75 years beneath the roundabout had to be started in order to lower the water level some 400 yards away.

The Loddon's main source was in West Basingstoke where, in my younger days, Spring Pond was enclosed by high banks. In the spring, the water would rise 40 feet to flood the fields farmed by the Rendell family. In the town, there is a spring near Bramblys Drive which, many years ago, flooded Mortimer Lane, making a ford to cross at the bottom of Sarum Hill. It is a fact that in the 18th century, wild bird fowling took place where the New Inn stands today.

The worst floods in the Brookvale area occurred some 80 years ago when the water from the spring at Spring Pond and another at Buckskin, where Cairngorm Close is today, turned the water meadows where Mr Rendell grazed his cattle into a large lake. In those days, part of the River Loddon in King George's meadow behind the former Thornycroft works had not been conduited. Water flowed through the culvert beneath the high embankment along which trains ran on the

Basingstoke and Alton Light Railway and flooded the field, parts of George Street and Lower Brook Street, before flowing back into the main stream at the bottom of Queen's Road. In George Street and Lower Brook Street planks had to be laid for people to cross the road.

The pumps in the Victory roundabout were placed there over 100 years ago to drain the cellars of several public houses, namely the Victory, New Inn, the Rose, the Barge and the Railway Inn. Today, the river runs in the open through Glebe Gardens, before it is conduited beneath the lower parts of the town centre after which it again runs in the open. By the time it reaches the water meadows at Old Basing, the Loddon is quite wide. It then flows on through Sherfield-on-Loddon, eventually running into the Thames to the east of Reading.

The Brookvale area has been spared flooding in recent years through the deepening of the bore hole at West Ham waterworks to meet the needs of Basingstoke's great influx of people. Today, the waterworks can no longer supply water for the 100,000 or more residents, and the local water source is supplemented from wells at Lasham, near Alton and from the Thames at Sunbury.

There is no doubt that the subterranean channels feeding the Loddon are linked with those feeding the River Test, which actually rises to the west of the Beach Arms, Oakley. By the time the Test reaches Overton, it is quite wide. For many years, before improved drainage was constructed, the spring in Cairngorm Close regularly flooded the Worting Road at Worting Bottom. A piece of land was sold for a bungalow to be built, and the first year after it was completed and the new owners had moved in, the springs rose and the water came up through the floorboards. To overcome the nuisance, a moat was dug around the bungalow and drain pipes were laid. The owners of the property were far from pleased.

The River Loddon used to flow under Coppyn Bridge at the bottom of Church Street, then under the boys' playground of St John's school and alongside a path to Wote Street. Here, it ran alongside the now demolished Jackson's Garage before running to the rear of the erstwhile Basingstoke Steam Laundry, under Eastrop Lane and out toward Old Basing.

In centuries past, much of the town's sewage ran into the Loddon. Waste ran down the gutters in New Street and Church Street, and platforms were built for people to walk on. At one time the river was

Floods in Winchester Road following a storm.

used as a privy and the vicar of Basingstoke himself was fined for committing such an offence. One hundred or so years later, the Loddon's waters were so clean that trout could be seen in what is now Glebe Gardens. It was necessary to lay fishnets to prevent the trout getting into the lower shallow reaches. People used to catch trout and other fish by leaning over Coppyn Bridge in Church Street, close to where the entrance is now to Chute House.

Today, you can hear part of the River Loddon flowing beneath Churchill Way, built on what was Brook Street. Years ago there was a ford where Churchill Way passes through the tunnel under the new town centre.

SPORT

A S IN MANY other small towns, organised sport in Basingstoke did not really get underway until the beginning of the 20th century. In Basingstoke, however, Lt-Col John May's gift of the Folly to the town resulted in competitive cricket being played in late Victorian times. In addition to cricket, the Folly was big enough to accommodate a cycle track, and later a hockey pitch. Before the Folly was given to the town, good class cricket, mainly amateur, was played at Hackwood Park.

Football in Basingstoke began to become popular in Edwardian times, with matches played on Basingstoke Common. One of the crack teams was the North Hants Ironworks, who were more of a match for the first Basingstoke Town Football Club. One of the leading junior clubs was the Thistle, their matches also being played on the common.

As Basingstoke Town progressed, they obtained a ground at Jayes Meadow, near the Golden Lion Inn on the Basingstoke by-pass. In an age of little public transport, it was a long way for supporters to go, and many used bicycles to get there. Eventually, Basingstoke Town were able to play on Castle Field to the south of the Folly, then known as May's Bounty. At Castle Field there was a large stand with enclosed changing rooms. This is where, as a young teenager, I first saw Hampshire County League football. On the east side of the field was Cannon's Meadow where cattle grazed. In 1930, Basingstoke was still a market town, and the grazing cattle were evidence of it.

In those days there was strong rivalry between Basingstoke Town and Thornycroft's, both playing in the same league. For playing conditions, Thornycroft were by far the better equipped, having three football pitches at West Ham Park, a fine stand and a suitable venue for semi-finals of the Hampshire Senior Cup. Thornycroft's had a full-time groundsman in Mr Jack Moore, a former Hampshire County cricket player. He had also played both football and cricket for the Thornycroft Athletic Club. He also provided pitches for rugby and hockey, tennis courts and an excellent bowling green. When World War Two broke out, organised sport was greatly curtailed. Thornycroft lost its football stand as the area was required for a gun shop.

Fairfields Recreation Ground boasted fine tennis courts as well as an excellent bowling green and pavilion, and the ground still flourishes today. In recent years Hampshire County Cricket Club have had a very successful cricket week at May's Bounty. Such a popular event ended in the 2000 millennium season when the cricket club moved to a new county ground at Southampton.

In recent years, a fine sporting complex has been provided at Down Grange, close to Kempshott, where the Basingstoke Rugby Club usually runs three fifteens.

Goldings Park was the site of a bowling green, tennis courts and a football pitch for nearly 70 years. Bowls are no longer played there and the tennis courts have been moved to part of Basingstoke Common.

Basingstoke has had a fine reputation for its boxing. At the end of World War One, the town had a challenger for the world heavyweight title in John Beckett who, in his fight with the French Carpentier, was outclassed. In the years between the wars, extending into the 1950s, Basingstoke had a stable of professional boxers such as Vince Hawkins and Gardiner, the heavyweight boxer, both managed by local man, John Simpson.

The town also had a highly successful boxing club which produced boxers who won several titles. Fred Simpson, son of the boxing manager, fought as a Fairfields schoolboy in the Golden Gloves

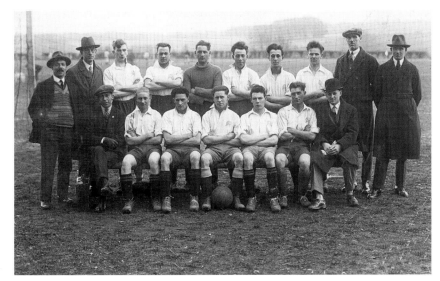

Basingstoke Leather Works football team, 1927–28.

Basingstoke Football Club.

competition in New York and won his bout. He continued and eventually held the lightweight title of Great Britain.

When Basingstoke had so many boxers, bouts were arranged at Thornycroft's canteen, in Worting Road, drawing boxers from a wide area, including many army boxers.

Basingstoke has lost many acres of farmland during the past 75 years, mostly to industrial development. However, most of what was Rendell's West Ham Farm has now been taken for leisure purposes, with a ten-pin bowling alley, an ice rink where national ice hockey is played and many of the United Kingdom's top figure skaters have performed, and an indoor bowling green. There is also a nine-hole golf course to supplement the well-known Basingstoke and North Hampshire Golf Course at Kempshott. There are other golf courses in the Basingstoke area at Dummer, Park Prewett and Tadley.

There was a golf course at Oakridge until 1921 when the course was opened at Kempshott. The golf course at Oakridge was earmarked for use as an airfield and, at the time, it was possible that Basingstoke could have an air terminal. When plans to build an airport at Heathrow were announced, the site at Oakridge, which was by this time being used for private light aircraft, was developed and houses were built.

As regards indoor sports, Basingstoke has a fine sports centre in the new town centre which includes a very well-used swimming pool.

Crowds turn out to watch a
Showbiz XI, with Tommy Steele
(centre) play at Camrose Ground.

Before it was built Basingstoke's only facility for swimming was the
open-air swimming pool at West Ham, the site of which is now the
centre of the Thornycroft roundabout.

JOHN ARLOTT

ONE OF Basingstoke's best known sons was John Arlott, who was
internationally known as a cricket commentator for the BBC. For a man
who was not a professional cricketer, his knowledge of the game and of
those who played it was second to none. He is remembered, not just for
his descriptive technique, but for his Hampshire burr.

John Arlott's father was a cemetery superintendent and it was at the
Victorian cemetery lodge at Chapel Hill that he was born. His father
had been superintendent of what many folk used to refer to as the 'old
cemetery'. When his father was appointed superintendent of the new
cemetery at Worting Road, the lodge he occupied at Chapel Hill became
empty and he made an application for the lodge for his son. The request
was granted.

John started school at Fairfields and gained a scholarship. He then
attended Queen Mary's School, then situated in Worting Road, in the
days when Mr Percival was Headmaster. On leaving school, John took
a post with Basingstoke Borough Council at the municipal buildings. He
then took a post in the administration section of Park Prewett Hospital.

At that time, his only knowledge of cricket was with local teams such as Sherborne St John and the hospital.

Eventually, he joined the Southampton Constabulary and it was when on duty at the County Ground, Southampton that he played in his only county match, being asked to field as twelfth man. A well-read man, he entered the field of sports journalism and, for a time, was on the staff of the *London Evening News*. He took a post with the BBC and became a cricket commentator, sharing the reporting box with famous cricketers, mostly those who had been capped for England and Australia.

A powerful writer, he became a poet and a connoisseur of wines. He also wrote hymns, one of which is often sung in churches today. Interested in politics, he came from a Liberal family and stood for that persuasion in a general election.

For many years his home was at Alresford, Hampshire, but he finally made Alderney in the Channel Islands his retirement home. He was a well-travelled man who very rarely missed a test match in England, the West Indies, South Africa, Australia and New Zealand.

As a scholar of Queen Mary's School, he shared the honour of being an old boy of that school with Gilbert White, author of the *Natural History of Selborne*.

WINTERS OF OLD

GLOBAL WARMING could have dire consequences if left unchecked, and already in Basingstoke changes in climate are apparent. The young people of today have never known snow of the kind that we used to endure. The *Basingstoke Gazette*, which has recorded the history of Basingstoke for over 125 years, provides many examples of snowfalls so deep that they brought transport to a standstill and cut many villages off.

After the Christmas of 1962, from Boxing Day to 4 January 1963, Basingstoke suffered four very heavy snowfalls followed by a seven-week big freeze. It was not until mid-February that a thaw set in. Headlines in the *Gazette* said it was the worst freeze-up for 80 years. One of the areas to be badly affected by blizzards was Kingsclere Road, with snowdrifts eight feet high in places. One photograph in the *Gazette* showed a sign post pointing to the village of Ramsdell almost buried in a drift.

This was the blizzard in which a coach load of passengers, returning from a theatre trip to Oxford, had to spend the night in the coach when it became stuck in a drift near Hannington. Another coach was stuck in a drift near Ellisfield and had to be abandoned. It was no joke for the passengers who had to walk over three miles to Cliddesden. Despite the efforts of workmen to try and keep roads open, the Wilts and Dorset Omnibus Company could only operate town services and suspended the country services. Families living at Whitedown, near Wootton St Lawrence, were snowbound from Saturday 30 December 1962 until the following Wednesday. Tufton GP, Dr R.H. Walker, made two mercy flights in an Army Air Corps helicopter from Middle Wallop to reach two of his patients, one at

London Road after a snowstorm.

Snowdrifts on the road near Park Prewett, 1958.

a bungalow on the outskirts of Whitchurch and the other at the appropriately named Frost Hill Farm, near Overton.

One casualty of the heavy snowfalls was a Basingstoke-based steam locomotive that had to be sent to the breakers yard. The loco, 0-6-0 Drummond '700' Class No.30368, built in 1897, was fitted with a snow plough for clearing the lines. While engaged in clearing the Basingstoke to Salisbury line, it developed a hot axle box and was deemed a failure. Consequently, it was towed back to Basingstoke and lingered, minus its snow plough, in a siding for several months, awaiting its final journey.

Schools could not re-open until 16 January 1963. My son, Robin, then a 14-year-old schoolboy, recalls running his school cross-country course and finding himself actually running on the hedge tops where the snow was so deep. Country One edition of the *Gazette* showed a picture of Mr F. Barrington driving a Drott shovel through walls of snow in an attempt to keep the road to Wootton St Lawrence open. The last blizzard of the prolonged freeze-up occurred on Wednesday 6 February. In the issue of 22 February, the *Gazette* reported that Hampshire County Council had spent £550,000 on clearing and gritting the county's roads and repairing frost damage.

Another severe snowfall I remember was in 1926, when Basingstoke was covered by at least a foot of snow. I can remember being shown telegraph poles almost buried in huge drifts at the bottom of Common Hill on London Road. In order to reach his customers at Kite Hill, Old Kempshott Lane, the Thornton's Bakery roundsman had to take his horse from the shafts, sling baskets of bread across the animal and lead it through a narrow cutting made in huge drifts which had blocked the road between Worting and Five Ways, Kempshott. Sherborne Road was also blocked with drifts between three and four feet high. All Aldershot & District Traction bus services were cancelled. The railway was also badly affected and was blocked in several places in the Alton, Winchester and Eastleigh areas, making rail travel from Basingstoke extremely difficult.

One has only to go back over 150 years to the pages of Samuel Attwood's diary to read of extreme weather conditions, cases of which were frequently recorded until the diary's last entries of 1870. The winter of 1829–1830 must have been particularly severe, for Samuel Attwood wrote that he could not get to work for several days. He was a tailor and lost three days work in December 1829 and another five

New Street, looking toward Victoria Street. Most of the shops here were demolished in the years after World War Two.

days in January 1830. On 7 February 1830 he wrote, 'Could not get to work for four and a half days owing to the severe frost and snow'. Amazingly, he wrote six weeks later, on 21 March, 'Very hot weather – I never remember such in my life for this time of the year', and yet a week later he wrote, 'Very cold weather'. As if to play an April Fools Day trick after the hot spell, Samuel Attwood entered in his diary for 1 April 1830, 'Snow on the ground, two inches deep'.

When my father was a young man in late Victorian days, he saw people skating on the Basingstoke Canal between the wharf at Eastrop and the Broadwater at Old Basing.

My grandfather's uncle, Samuel Attwood, also enjoyed his skating for he wrote in his diary in February, 1855, 'An extraordinary severe winter with a great quantity of snow. I went sliding six times on the Basingstoke Canal and twice on Hackwood Park Basin up to February 22nd. February 16th was the coldest day and night for very many years'. He also went sliding at Hackwood Park in December 1859.

In 1881, three years after the *Gazette* first appeared, many parts of the country had a severe snowstorm and the paper reported that large

Soldiers clearing snow outside
Lansing Bagnall, Kingsclere Road,
1952.

heaps of snow lined the streets of Basingstoke. The report said that the snowstorm in the Basingstoke neighbourhood had not been so disastrous as in many parts of the country where the loss of life had been appalling. The *Gazette* also said: As a proof of the severity of the frost we may allude to the circumstance of the sheep being roasted on the Thames at Twickenham. In our youthful days we heard and read with wonder of the bullock roasted by the Londoners, but never till now have we heard of a similar occurrence in our own history. Should the weather continue to be as rigorous as at the present time, it is not improbable that we may hear of other animals being cooked on the frozen surface of the Thames. Would that thousands of fat beasts could be slaughtered and dressed for the starving multitudes of Londoners. In a small town, a society like we have in Basingstoke may be able to grapple with poverty and misery aggravated by the severe weather.

The *Gazette* carried a story concerning two Basingstoke men who lost their way when crossing fields off the Sherborne Road, which was blocked by drifts and nearly lost their lives. By chance, they spotted a light in a farmhouse where they were taken in for the night. The London and South Western Railway, however, did a roaring trade in issuing tickets for Fleet, where the pond attracted many skaters from stations at Oakley, Aldershot and Basingstoke, from where 80 return tickets were issued on the Saturday. Ice hockey was played on the pond where several acres of frozen water were swept for the skaters. 'The continued frost has had the effect of improving the skating of the Basingstoke ladies and much of the nervousness, which once characterised their efforts, has vanished', a newspaper report read.

Some made money out of the skaters, for the price of an afternoon's enjoyment was 1s 6d train fare, a tip for the sweeper and either 2s or 2s 6d for the man putting on the skates.

The *Gazette* suggested to the town authorities the desirability of moving the snow from the streets lest a sudden thaw should cause serious flooding at the bottom of Church Street and Wote Street. The suggestion was also made that the snow should be carted to the common or some other open space, but 'in Newbury, the snow is being thawed by a steam engine'.

As a comforting thought, many people say in March 'that spring is only just around the corner'. This is what they said in 1908, only to become disillusioned in the last Saturday in April when the *Gazette* said: 'The snowstorm will probably be remembered for many years to come to have been of exceptional severity such as the great snowstorm of January 1881 and which can hardly be compared with the snowstorms of Derby Day, 1867'.

The snow began to fall at breakfast time with flakes 'as large as half-crowns' and continued throughout the day. Business in the town was completely at a standstill. On the Sunday, a snowplough of primitive design, drawn by three horses, was used to clear the streets. The council's regular staff was supplemented by 40 extra men. All those engaged in the work of clearing the street were given breakfast at the Old Angel Café in the Market Place on the Monday. On the same day, the snowplough was used at Kempshott to clear the way for a 100hp car from Brooklands. Snowdrifts had made the road impassable and traffic was diverted.

The villages around Basingstoke were completely snowed up, with 16 inches on the level at Kingsclere. Trains were stopped at Oakley

Snowdrifts at Battledown.

because of the snow putting signals out of action. The Overton carrier, Mr Glasspool, was unable to reach Basingstoke after his horse fell. But the blizzard did not prevent a wedding from taking place at Wootton St Lawrence, where there were drifts of eight feet. The rural postmen had great difficulty in completing their rounds on the Saturday and several had to spend the night in the villages as it was impossible to return to Basingstoke.

HOUSING

NO ATTEMPT to give Basingstoke a pattern of housing was made until the latter part of Queen Victoria's reign, when what was called New Town was built in west Basingstoke. Many houses were built in May Street and Lower Brook Street, two up and two down, with no inside toilets. The latter were at the top of a small back garden, which was most inconvenient in bad weather. The houses in Lower Brook Street had front doors which opened out on to the pavements, whereas those in May Street had very small front gardens.

Efforts were made to make the area self-supporting, with premises for general stores included in the planning. There were 200 houses in May Street and about 40 in Brook Street. All were demolished in the 1960s and the residents rehoused in new housing areas.

May Street and Brook Street formed a very close-knit community and it took time for the old Basingstoke folk to become integrated with Basingstoke's newcomers, who were mostly Londoners. There were houses dotted about Basingstoke, with many old dwellings in the

Chapel Street cottages in the 19th century.

Basingstoke's first council houses, Cranbourne Lane, built in 1914 and demolished in 1966.

Reading Road area and in the vicinity of the railway station. In my childhood days, there were still a few thatched cottages around, but today there is only one left, at Worting.

A modern design of house was built toward the end of the 19th century in the Essex Road area and after Thornycroft's plant was opened, the Brookvale area was built, with several shops, again to make the area self-supporting. There was some development in the Norn Hill area at the beginning of the 20th century and if Lord Bolton had succeeded, what we know as the South View area, leading into Oakridge, would have become a private housing estate, with long gardens. Planning permission was refused, however, but strangely the plans survived and 50 years later the borough of Basingstoke developed the whole area almost to Lord Bolton's plans, the main thoroughfare being Queen Mary Avenue.

By this time, the borough had turned its attention to local authority housing and during World War One, Basingstoke's first council houses were built in Cranbourne Lane. These were the first of the town's council houses to be demolished when the site was required to build the King's Furlong neighbourhood shopping centre in the early 1970s.

Basingstoke's crooked house in the lower part of town, now demolished.

During the latter part of World War One, Basingstoke Borough Council commenced a large council home development with the building of Sherborne Road, Kingsclere Road, Lancaster Road and Merton Road, the latter being completed in the 1920s. At this time, two more schemes were commenced, namely, the South Ham estate to the west of the town and the Grove Road estate to the south. The roads on this estate were named Grove Road, Hackwood Road and Chesterfield Road, the latter named after a mayor of Basingstoke. Local authority home building in Basingstoke then slowed down, the exception being the South Ham estate, where homes continued to be built until the 1950s, with further expansion taking place in the 1960s.

The Overspill Agreement made between Basingstoke Borough Council, Hampshire County Council and London County Council, which increased the town's population from 26,000 to 85,000 and eventually, 100,000, saw a tripartite arrangement for the allocation of local authority housing, with one in four of every new house being allocated to a Basingstoke family.

The first estate to be constructed under the Overspill Agreement was the Oakridge area, which included houses built in the 1950s for employees of the Atomic Weapons Research Establishment (AWRE) at nearby Aldermaston. This estate occupies the west of the area. The main Oakridge area occupies both sides of the Reading Road and to the north

Ford's buildings, which stood close to the Victory roundabout, 1823.

of Queen Mary Avenue. From Oakridge, development moved to north-west Basingstoke, adjoining the Houndmill industrial estate, with Sainsbury's distribution depot the largest industrial complex in the area. For many years, it adjoined the Lansing Bagnall fork-lift truck plant. The area chosen for local authority housing for the employees of the various companies located at Houndmill was Winklebury, which for many years appeared to be waste land, dotted with poultry farms and with one building of substance, namely Winklebury House. The owners of the poultry farms and some of their employees lived in disused railway carriages converted into dwellings, which gave the area the appearance of a ghost railway marshalling yard. Today, the Winklebury estate has a secondary school, two junior and infant schools and a new church.

With the development of Winklebury, houses for the newcomers stretched as far west as the top of Kempshott Hill. It was to include much of Worting village, the large Buckskin estate and the private developments in Kempshott and the Berg estate. The latter adjoins the South Ham estate, to make a sea of housing between Worting Road and Winchester Road. Houses built on the Winchester Road side had the advantage of an industrial estate between Winchester Road and Cranbourne Lane. The industrial estate was the home of the extensive Smith's Industries plant, which has been rebuilt on a much smaller scale, releasing land which is now occupied by retail stores and fast-food outlets.

Farm House, Church Street, site of the Hospital of St John, 1840.

Old House at Home Inn, Bunnian Place, with its thatched roof, before it was the scene of a fire.

View from the railway bridge looking down Chapel Street in the 1920s.

To the south of the old Basingstoke by-pass lies the extensive area of Brighton Hill, which has been further extended by development at Hatch Warren where, situated in the centre, is a large Sainsbury's superstore. The Brighton Hill area has a secondary school and a number of junior and infant schools. In addition, there are three churches.

To the north of Brighton Hill, between Cranbourne Lane and Cliddesden Road, is the Harrow Way estate, which has local shopping facilities and the town's only Church of England junior and infant school.

The town has also been developed to the east and south-east. The old village of Eastrop is now a large area of private housing, but minuscule when compared to the private housing developments at Chineham. After falling almost into obscurity from the mediaeval days when it had a squire, life has returned to Chineham in a big way. It has a flourishing neighbourhood shopping centre and is separated from Basingstoke by an industrial estate, mainly populated by small companies.

To complete the new Basingstoke, there is the town's painters' area – the Black Dam estate, part of which has been built on what was formerly known as the Little Common. The housing extends from what

was Basingstoke Common to the M3 motorway. An attempt to give the area a neighbourhood shopping centre has not been very successful. The Black Dam estate has a junior and infant school and has a rather beautiful recreational area, complete with water birds and pond life.

It is still difficult to find affordable housing in Basingstoke, and much more development is bound to occur. I am sure the time will come when the green belt between Basingstoke and Sherborne St John will be overrun by housing. As it is, there is very little open country between Bramley and Sherborne St John. It would appear that the M3 acts as a barrier to the south of the town, preventing any further large-scale development from taking place.

TOWN DEVELOPMENT

BASINGSTOKE must lay claim to being the town which, in a remarkably short space of time, underwent changes greater and more drastic than any other town in Great Britain. Within 35 years, the overspill scheme, designed to move thousands of people out of London, has raised the population from 30,000 to approximately 100,000. This was the result of an agreement made under the 1952 Town Development Act between the London County Council, Hampshire County Council and Basingstoke Borough Council.

The scheme was to change a small market town into an important business area, a change which would affect the culture and the nature of employment, with the old manual industries being superseded by the computer age. In this chapter I will seek to explain this extraordinary change in the town's history and to illustrate the many buildings, streets and districts that were altered, demolished or transformed.

Such changes are nothing new, for in their report to Parliament in 1837 – the year Queen Victoria came to the throne – the Commissioners for Municipal Corporations Boundaries said of Basingstoke:

Stooked corn in a field opposite Eastrop Church, which is now part of the Eastrop estate.

the town is represented to be gradually increasing in size and importance. It contains no manufactories, but is a place of very great thoroughfare and is situated in the centre of a rich agricultural district. The markets here are well attended, being resorted to by persons from Andover, Winchester, Newbury and Reading.

By the end of the 19th century, Basingstoke, as an agricultural town, was on the wane. Manufacturing concerns such as Burberry's, John May, Thornycroft's and Wallis & Steevens were already established in the town. However, the town clung on to its agricultural roots for at

The Black Boy (now the Hop Leaf) in Victorian times.

least another 60 years, with a thriving cattle market and both arable and livestock farming continuing on the outskirts.

The 1921 census of population recorded that primary industries such as farming, market gardening and nurseries employed 300, manufacturing 2,400 and service trades 3,070. Agriculture, however, continued to remain the mainstay of the local economy, accounting for

Junction Road – all the houses were later demolished to make way for road developments.

Looking west along Brook Street while preparations were being made for building Churchill Way.

Demolition of Wallis & Steevens' Station Hill engineering plant.

75 per cent of the labour force in the rural districts around Basingstoke.

How well I remember those days when, on a Wednesday, the cattle market outside the railway station had stalls crowded with animals, many of them destined for the slaughter houses of the town. For me, it was a grim sight to see bullocks and sheep being driven through the streets on their last journey.

All this ceased when the overspill scheme came into effect, and literally half of the town centre was bulldozed. The market stalls and most of the slaughter houses were casualties, as were 18 public houses and many shops.

The old folk were saddened to see their shopping places consigned to the flames, while businessmen were in conflict with the authorities over the low prices offered under compulsory purchase orders.

Not only shops were reduced to piles of rubble. Georgian buildings

Basingstoke was a horticultural centre until modern development began in the 1960s. These two photographs show Jordan's Nurseries, Winchester Road, in 1930.

such as Brook House, Queen Anne House and the Friends Meeting House were ruthlessly destroyed. More important was the destruction of hundreds of homes where, often, generations of families had lived for 80 years. Whole communities were broken up in this way, and to be ordered to quit one's house and move to a new estate, not necessarily close to old neighbours and family members, was very hard to bear.

Densely populated areas such as May Street and Brook Street were required for new roads, some of which passed through former allotments. But further disappointments lay ahead, with the closing down of the older industries such as Wallis & Steevens, Thornycroft's, the Basingstoke Joint Nurseries and, surprisingly, the railways, which in the days of steam had employed more than 250 workers.

Many new companies moved in under the overspill scheme, but often the new jobs on offer were only suitable for the younger workers. Two companies to move into the town during the last 65 years were Lansing Linde, fork-lift truck makers, and Eli Lilly, manufacturers of pharmaceutical products. For office workers, the Automobile Association at Fanum House and other locations in the town has provided

Staff employed at the Nurseries.

Brook House, Brook Street, by the entrance to the Churchill Way site of the first Basingstoke High School for Girls. This fine town house was a casualty of the 1960s development.

many opportunities for local people. Initially, the AA transferred many of their London-based staff to Basingstoke.

Another organisation to take over one of the high-rise office buildings in the town was the Civil Service Commission. When the commission first moved to Basingstoke, many of their workers were transferred from London. However, the commission vacated their imposing building during the early part of the last decade and it has now been demolished.

Basingstoke has a large commuting population with hundreds travelling by rail to London daily. Other workers commute in great numbers to Aldermaston, some eight miles north of Basingstoke, to work at AWE.

To expand, as was the case at Basingstoke, or to build an entirely new town involves hospital provision, many new schools, improved highways and hundreds of new homes on new estates. In Basingstoke, these are at Oakridge, Popley, Winklebury, Buckskin, the Berg, Kempshott, South Ham, Brighton Hill, Black Dam, Hatch Warren and Chineham. The increase in population of the Basingstoke area has also required the provision of a crematorium at North Waltham.

The new areas include local shopping areas and community centres. At the time of the Queen's Silver Jubilee in 1977, it was those people

Eli Lilly's pharmaceutical plant and offices.

Demolition of St John's School in the 1960s.

Church Street, 1936.

North of the town centre in the mid-1960s. Almost all the buildings, except the railway station and the inn behind it, were demolished.

Stalls at Basingstoke's livestock
market.

from London living on estates such as Popley who showed what it was
to celebrate, holding elaborate street parties complete with fancy dress,
flags and other decorations.

The Civil Service Commission was not the only large organisation to
leave Basingstoke. A number of others have left the Houndmills and
Winchester Road industrial estates.

One major change in recent years was the closing and subsequent

Steam Dell, Reading Road, where the first Basingstoke waterworks were. It continued in use until 1904.

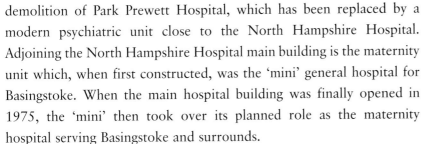

demolition of Park Prewett Hospital, which has been replaced by a modern psychiatric unit close to the North Hampshire Hospital. Adjoining the North Hampshire Hospital main building is the maternity unit which, when first constructed, was the 'mini' general hospital for Basingstoke. When the main hospital building was finally opened in 1975, the 'mini' then took over its planned role as the maternity hospital serving Basingstoke and surrounds.

The last sale at Basingstoke cattle
market.

Lower Wote Street before the
days of development in the
1960s.

Potter's Lane being demolished.

Kingsclere Road, Basingstoke, 1912. The Holy Ghost Roman Catholic church, which stands in the centre of the photograph, is now on the southern edges of the housing development.

Demolition scene at Wote Street.

The Shrubbery – home of Mr Burberry (of rain-coat fame) and later Basingstoke's first maternity home, in Cliddesden Road.

Harrow public house in Church Street, which closed in Edwardian times. Chute house stands behind the site of the pub

Pumping station, Basing Road.

The Rose and Crown, Church Street, built in 1692 and demolished in the 1960s.

Tree-lined Sarum Hill in the early 1920s. This is one of the few Victorian streets in Basingstoke that has survived modern development.

Pre-development photograph of
Wote Street showing the Waldorf
cinema, which opened in 1935.

Some of the houses in May Street,
Basingstoke's longest street with
200 houses, now demolished.

Public Library and Museum, New
Street, 1940.

Bottom of Wote Street, showing the Reformer's tree, horse trough and 'Isle of Man', as the gent's toilet was called.

Eastrop parochial church hall, opposite the bottom of New Road, which was demolished around 1970.

Down Grange House off Winchester Road, now a restaurant.

The Market Place in 1935.

Assembly Rooms to the south of the Market Square, where Jane Austen used to dance. They were demolished in the 1970s.

John Mares' tailoring factory, New Street.

Basingstoke Power Station, Brook Street, in 1967 prior to demolition.

Cross Street, Basingstoke, 1960.

Basing Road sheepwash, a favourite haunt of many children.

SHOPS THAT WERE

O LDER BASINGSTOKE people still have vivid memories of the Basingstoke they knew in their younger days, such as going to Aylward's photographers at the top of Wote Street to see their wedding photograph displayed. They might possibly have visited Kemps, further down Wote Street, to buy a gown, and some may even remember signing on the dole at the Labour Exchange during the slump between the wars.

Shoppers in Wote Street will remember buying shoes from Mr Jeffries or going along Potters Lane to buy paints and wallpapers from Munfords. It was in Wote Street that many couples were married at the Basingstoke Register Office opposite the Grapes Inn, and they would have been to Brigg's shop a few days before to buy the wedding ring.

In those days, there was a large shop in Wote Street named Tyrrell, Smith and Gripper with a large grocery and cake department, quite close to the Immanuel Church of the Countess of Huntingdon's Connexion. This church was one of the first that the countess opened after severing her support of the Church of England in Bath. During its

Nutts stationery shop, Church Street.

Punter's popular ironmongery and tool shop, Wote Street.

Looking down New Street.

The Kiosk restaurant in the Market Square.

final years, the small congregation came from only one or two families.

Wote Street will also bring back memories of going to Mr Grubb's dentistry with toothache or buying delicious cakes from Giles bakers shop. It was where John M. Carter had his tent and rope shop and the headquarters of his flourishing tent hire business.

There was Mr Compton, the dairyman, who before the days of refrigerators made two deliveries daily during the hot weather to supply fresh milk. There were the two Miss Philpotts in Potters Lane with their second-to-none home-made cake shop next door to the Rose and Crown Inn, which had the date of its building, 1692, displayed over the door. Old pubs such as that meant nothing to the planners who ordered the bulldozers to commence their work of devastation, much to the sorrow of the old inhabitants.

Ask any local senior citizen which they prefer, the old or the new Basingstoke, and they will very likely say the old. Younger townsfolk knew that great sweeping changes had to be made to bring modernity to Basingstoke and to have larger shops to meet the needs of the throngs of newcomers. At the time, a move was afoot to make nearby Hook the

New Street, looking toward Victoria Street.

overspill town; if that had happened, Basingstoke would have become very much the poor relation. As it was, landowners who had vested interests used their influence against the planners to retain Hook as an expanding village. Since those days, however, it has attracted pockets of commerce and industry, considerable housing development and has a large supermarket.

The top of Wote Street and Church Street in Basingstoke escaped the bulldozers, with the Black Boy, now the Hop Leaf, remaining a popular pub. It goes back several centuries and at one time was owned by my forbears.

Opposite the Hop Leaf was the Moose Hall, previously the Baptist Church. When the building was demolished, the baptismal pit was found, still intact, under the floor. Next to the Moose Hall was, at one time, a fascinating shop by the name of the Little Dustman, which sold a remarkable range of goods, including liquidated stock and fire

The Warren, Church Street. George Stevens' newsagents.

Ody's grocery shop in Edwardian times.

Watson's garage, Wote Street, which faced the lower Market Place.

Wote Street and Station Hill, 1920.

salvage. The last proprietor, Mr W. Aston, also sold birds and animals, including monkeys. In the 1930s the business suffered a serious fire, causing all the animals and birds to perish. The Little Dustman dated back to late Victorian times.

An old part of Basingstoke, still partially intact, is Cross Street, where

the Basingstoke Heritage Society erected a statue of a Blue Coat schoolboy on the site of the old school. Among the paving stones have been placed some record of Basingstoke's history, which shows that Basingstoke does make an effort to encourage culture. Cross Street and Upper Church Street are now pedestrian areas, as are London Street and Winchester Street. The furniture shop of Vernon Griffiths and Griffins the butchers in Church Street are now just memories.

The White Hart Inn, London Road in an old-world setting. Today it is surrounded by modern development.

From 1878 until 1972 the *Basingstoke Gazette*'s office was in Church Street, with the printing works behind the shop. Access to the printing works was obtained from Windover Street. The *Basingstoke Gazette*, formerly the *Hants & Berks Gazette*, has files extending back to the first copies. These can be seen on microfiche in the Basingstoke branch of the Hampshire County Library.

The news items from the Victorian period onwards give a miniature history of old Basingstoke. The advertisements, too, can be most

Church Street, 1910.

The Warren newspaper shop in Church Street, kept by George Stevens.

fascinating. During the last 25 years of Victoria's reign, dentistry was coming into fashion, with travelling dentists advertising in the *Gazette* the address from which they would be operating, often a cake shop or a butchers. This meant that you could buy a lardy cake or sausages at the front of the shop and see teeth being drawn out at the back.

Sometimes the travelling dentist would bring his own horse-drawn caravan. The

Church Street, 1918.

Basingstoke Market Place, 1920.

Victorian History of Hampshire shows a caravan in Basingstoke Market Square being used as a dentist's surgery. An accompanying German band would strike up as soon as a client entered the caravan, a novel way of ensuring that 'It was painless dentistry' as advertised. The name of the dentist over the front of the caravan was 'Squelah'. My father related this story to me when I was a boy, but I must confess that I did not believe it until I saw it in print with a photograph.

In the days of the 1920s and 1930s, Basingstoke was a town of small shopkeepers where one would normally receive personal attention. By the time the new shopping centre in Basingstoke is completed, more of the small private businesses in the town will have vanished.

Lower Wote Street before development.

The old silk mill building, Brook Street.

MODERN BASINGSTOKE

THE MILLENNIUM was a time of hope for Basingstoke, coinciding as it did with the commencement of the building of a shopping mall encompassing most of the eastern area of the old Basingstoke shopping centre. When completed, it will bring to Basingstoke a number of large stores to make the town competitive with neighbouring towns and cities such as Reading, Southampton and Winchester. It will have two towers to give the new project some originality.

Basingstoke entered the new millennium in a favourable economic situation with almost full employment. The local unemployment rate in spring 2001 was just 0.7%, the lowest in Great Britain. A wide variety of employment has brought many people to the town. One great problem remaining is that of the availability of affordable housing. Plans are being formulated to build housing estates outside the town

Basingstoke New Market Square, 1987. It is now just a memory.

Basingstoke shopping centre under construction.

The roundabout linking the A30 with the M3 under construction by the Black Dam.

and, in the case of Chineham, on the eastern side of Basingstoke. Plans are also in hand to build a railway station on the Basingstoke to Reading route, which has a frequent train service.

Although employment is high in the town, many people commute daily to London, Reading and Aldermaston. While the important phase

Part of the new Basingstoke Sun Life of Canada office block.

of the new Basingstoke is taking shape, business is being retarded in the present shops, several having closed down. One policy pursued by the Basingstoke and Deane Borough Council is neighbourhood shopping centres, where out-of-town supermarkets are attracting a lot of shoppers away from the town centre. Basingstoke has hundreds of chargeable parking spaces, whereas the supermarkets outside the town centre provide free parking. This is affecting the smaller shops who rely on the superstores to bring people into the centre of Basingstoke.

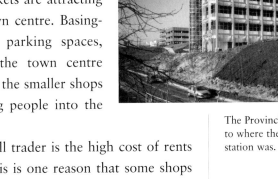

The Provincial Life building, close to where the railway goods station was.

Another problem faced by the small trader is the high cost of rents and business charges in the town. This is one reason that some shops have had to pull out of the town. It has not been all easy going for the major businesses that have moved into the town since the development of the 1960s and 1970s either. Quite a number have since moved elsewhere.

It was thought that with so many offices opening up, the need for commuting would tail off. In fact, it appears to be as popular as ever, with many people taking advantage of a frequent 43-minute rail service to Waterloo. Dominating the town in the east is the high-rise Fanum House, headquarters of the Automobile Association which also occupies other office blocks in the town. The Queen opened Fanum House in 1972 after which she went on a walk-about in Basingstoke town centre.

A great asset to the town is a sports centre within the town centre which has a swimming pool, planned just too small to accommodate international swimming events. In the early days of the sports centre, the main hall was used for indoor tennis, with international stars of tennis giving a demonstration of hard-court play, followed a few weeks later by an international match between Basingstoke and Czechoslovakia. The attempt to make Basingstoke a major centre for entertainment has been advanced with the opening of the Anvil, the ultra-modern concert hall near the railway station, attracting top entertainers and leading professional orchestras.

The counterpart of this popular attraction is the West Ham amusement park, pride of place being the ice-rink and, during the past few months, the very ambitious Milestones Transport Museum, which now also incorporates the Automobile Association museum. The museum has been very thoughtfully laid out and includes large replicas of part of Thornycroft's engineering works, with a number of restored vintage lorries and a splendid building showing Wallis & Steevens' Station Hill office block. The museum is so realistic that the huge overhead crane from Thornycroft's has been re-erected in working condition, but with a 1-ton lift restriction. Also incorporated in the museum is an inn and many authentic reproductions of everyday life, including the façades of some of the old shops of Basingstoke. It is a great asset to Basingstoke which will undoubtedly attract many visitors.

The new museum, built on former farmland, is within a quarter of a mile of the old Thornycroft site that is now a Safeway supermarket. The bridge underneath the railway, which was formerly used as farm access, is now used as a footpath and cycle track allowing access to Milestones and the West Ham Leisure Park.

General view from Eastrop.

Very little heavy engineering is left in Basingstoke nowadays, the main plant being Lansing Linde, which manufactures mechanical handling equipment. Formerly Lansing Bagnall, the company was taken over in recent years by a German firm which demolished the former plant and replaced it with one smaller but more efficient. Many acres once occupied by the former plant are now home to a diverse range of companies. The extensive J. Sainsbury distribution depot is adjacent, while opposite are Macmillan's offices and warehouse.

The Basingstoke branch of the Multiple Sclerosis Society in the grounds of Upton Grey House.

Much redevelopment is currently in progress on the old Park Prewett Hospital site, where many of the former ward buildings have been demolished and replaced by housing development. Part of the Park Prewett site is occupied by the North Hampshire Hospital complex.

Small light industrial developments have been built in the Basingstoke area on former farmland at Viables to the south of the town and Daneshill to the north-east. At one time the only industry in the latter area was a brickworks at Chineham, one of many within the Basingstoke area. There were also brickworks at Ramsdell and Nately Scures. Before the London Brick Company supplied thousands of bricks for the construction of the new Basingstoke, many of the town's buildings were built from local bricks.

In my lifetime, I have seen gas partly replaced by electricity, the town having been lit by gas since 1834 and by locally produced electricity since the days of World War One. There was an electricity generating station in Brook Street which supplied direct current. Electricity was supplied by the Borough of Basingstoke Electricity Department which was taken over by the Southern Electricity Board in the late 1940s when the supply of electricity was nationalised. However, the development of the national grid which distributed alternating current meant that by the end of the 1950s, Basingstoke was supplied with alternating current, the generating station being converted to the generation of alternating current only. The generating station had a maximum output of 4 megawatts and was switched in 'on load' at times of maximum demand. The generating station was closed and subsequently demolished by the early

1970s. Basingstoke also lost its gasworks and its associated gasholders, all of which were no longer required with the introduction of natural gas supplies from the North Sea. Also demolished was the town's sewerage pumping station in Basing Road, which was replaced by a modern waste treatment plant at Wildmoor, between Basingstoke and Sherfield-on-Loddon.

During the past 40 years, the town's healthcare provision has been transformed. In 1960 it consisted of the small Hackwood Road Cottage Hospital and the Basing Road Hospital, which catered for geriatrics and post-operative cases, with most emergency cases being taken to either Lord Mayor Treloar Hospital, Alton or the Royal Hampshire County Hospital, Winchester. Basingstoke now has the fine North Hampshire Hospital which was opened in 1975 and provides modern NHS care. The private healthcare needs of the area are serviced by the Hampshire Clinic on the site of Basing Road Hospital. This was originally the old Basingstoke Workhouse.

The other great change that has benefited the town is the modern road system. Some of the town centre streets have been pedestrianised and the M3 almost touches the town. The Basingstoke by-pass, built in 1930, which is part of the A30, is still very much in use, although part of its original route has been diverted over what was Basingstoke Common.

The common, once a popular open space, was taken over by a compulsory purchase order. An area on the east side of Basingstoke, skirting Old Basing, was transferred to the Common Trustees.

The removal of the common meant the end of common grazing of cattle and horses within the borough, and marked the final demise of the old market town of Basingstoke.

INDEX